NUTRITION & HEALTH

Food Regulation and Safety

NUTRITION & HEALTH

Food Regulation and Safety

KEVIN HILLSTROM

LUCENT BOOKS
A part of Gale, Cengage Learning

GALE
CENGAGE Learning·

Detroit • New York • San Francisco • New Haven, Conn • Waterville, Maine • London

LIBRARY OF CONGRESS CATALOGING-IN-PUBLICATION DATA

Hillstrom, Kevin, 1963-
  Food regulation and safety / by Kevin Hillstrom.
    p. cm. -- (Nutrition and health)
Summary: "Each title in the series delves into some of the hottest nutrition and health topics being discussed today. The series also provides readers with tools for evaluating conflicting and ever-changing ideas about nutrition and health"-- Provided by publisher.
  Includes bibliographical references and index.
  ISBN 978-1-4205-0721-8 (hardback)
1. Food--Safety measures--Juvenile literature. 2. Food contamination--Prevention--Juvenile literature.
  RA601.H55 2012
  363.19'2--dc23
                                                            2012002751

Lucent Books
27500 Drake Rd.
Farmington Hills, MI 48331

ISBN-13: 978-1-4205-0721-8
ISBN-10: 1-4205-0721-4

Printed in the United States of America
1 2 3 4 5 6 7 16 15 14 13 12

TABLE OF CONTENTS

Many people today are often amazed by the amount of nutrition and health information, often contradictory, that can be found in the media. Television, newspapers, and magazines bombard readers with the latest news and recommendations. Television news programs report on recent scientific studies. The healthy living sections of newspapers and magazines offer information and advice. In addition, electronic media such as websites, blogs, and forums post daily nutrition and health news and recommendations.

This constant stream of information can be confusing. The science behind nutrition and health is constantly evolving. Current research often leads to new ideas and insights. Many times, the latest nutrition studies and health recommendations contradict previous studies or traditional health advice. When the media reports these changes without giving context or explanations, consumers become confused. In a survey by the National Health Council, for example, 68 percent of participants agreed that "when reporting medical and health news, the media often contradict themselves, so I don't know what to believe." In addition, the Food Marketing Institute reported that eight out of ten consumers thought it was likely that nutrition and health experts would have a completely different idea about what foods are healthy within five years. With so much contradictory information, people have difficulty deciding how to apply nutrition and health recommendations to their lives. Students find it difficult to find relevant, yet clear and credible information for reports.

Changing recommendations for antioxidant supplements are an example of how confusion can arise. In the 1990s antioxidants such as vitamins C and E and beta-carotene came to the public's attention. Scientists found that people who ate more antioxidant-rich foods had a lower risk of heart disease, cancer, vision loss, and other chronic conditions than those who ate lower amounts. Without waiting for more scientific study, the media and supplement companies quickly spread the word that antioxidants could help fight and prevent disease. They recommended that people take antioxidant supplements and eat fortified foods. When further scientific studies were completed, however, most did not support the initial recommendations. While naturally occurring antioxidants in fruits and vegetables may help prevent a variety of chronic diseases, little scientific evidence proved antioxidant supplements had the same effect. In fact, a study published in the November 2008 *Journal of the American Medical Association* found that supplemental vitamins A and C gave no more heart protection than a placebo. The study's results contradicted the widely publicized recommendation, leading to consumer confusion. This example highlights the importance of context for evaluating nutrition and health news. Understanding a topic's scientific background, interpreting a study's findings, and evaluating news sources are critical skills that help reduce confusion.

Gale's Nutrition and Health series is designed to help young people sift through the mountain of confusing facts, opinions, and recommendations. Each book contains the most recent up-to-date information, synthesized and written so that students can understand and think critically about nutrition and health issues. Each volume of the series provides a balanced overview of today's hot-button nutrition and health issues while presenting the latest scientific findings and a discussion of issues surrounding the topic. The series provides young people with tools for evaluating conflicting and ever-changing ideas about nutrition and health. Clear narrative peppered with personal anecdotes, fully documented primary and secondary source quotes, informative sidebars, fact boxes, and statistics are all used to help readers understand these topics and how they affect their bodies and their lives. Each volume includes information about changes in trends over time, political controversies, and international perspectives. Full-color photographs and charts enhance all volumes in the series. The Nutrition and Health series is a valuable resource for young people to understand current topics and make informed choices for themselves.

Regulating America's Massive Food Delivery System

odern American families have a tremendous variety of foods to choose from when they visit a grocery store or restaurant. Store shelves and restaurant menus bulge with an eye-popping array of choices, from fancy cuts of domestically raised beef and pork to fruits and vegetables that originated hundreds or even thousands of miles away. America's kitchen pantries, school cafeterias, and restaurant stockrooms also feature an incredible assortment of prepackaged and processed foods, from bags of pretzels and cans of soup to frozen peas and popsicles.

Americans generally recognize that some of these foods are more nutritious and healthy than others, and many make their dietary selections based on those factors. Other Americans place a greater emphasis on personal taste, cost, and convenience when they decide where to dine or what to put in their grocery carts. The one consideration that rarely enters into their calculations is food safety. Most Americans take it for granted that all the foods and beverages they purchase are safe to consume.

For the most part, this faith in the safety of the nation's food supply is well-founded. Over the past century or so, government agencies at the local, state, and federal levels have crafted a complex web of food safety regulations and guidelines that have kept dangerous food-borne bacteria and other health threats at bay. These rules have been continually revised and updated over the years to keep up with amazing technological changes in the food industry. These changes have enabled the United States to generate huge volumes of cheap and tasty products on a daily basis.

In recent years, though, food safety has emerged as an issue of growing public concern. Deadly outbreaks of illness stemming from contaminated food sources have become an annual event in the United States. In addition, environmental and consumer advocacy groups charge that farms, ranches, and feedlots that make extensive use of pesticides, herbicides, and antibiotics are endangering public health and threatening fragile ecosystems. A heated national debate also has broken out over whether genetically modified (GM) crops and animals are safe for the environment and for human consumption.

A U.S. government official holds a bag of tomatoes being tested for salmonella during a nationwide outbreak in 2008. Contamination and other food safety issues are a growing public concern in the United States.

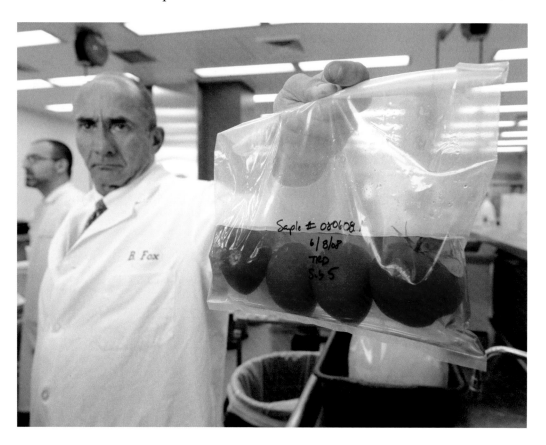

These controversies have led critics to claim that some sectors in America's mighty food industry are losing—or have already lost—their capacity to ensure the safety of their products. They believe that escalating food safety problems need to be addressed through new safety regulations and changes in industry practices. They also propose new educational campaigns to inform consumers about the potential health benefits and drawbacks of their food choices.

The food industry, however, opposes many of these proposed reforms. Food producers emphasize that tens of millions of Americans sit down for breakfast, lunch, dinner, and snacks every day without falling sick. Some farmers, feedlot owners, ranchers, food processors, grocery companies, and restaurant owners also argue that more stringent regulatory oversight will just increase their operating expenses—which will in turn force them to hike up the prices that consumers pay.

CHAPTER 1

The History of U.S. Food Safety

During colonial times and throughout most of America's first century of existence, regulations governing the raising, harvesting, preparation, and sale of crops, livestock, and other foodstuffs were rare. Early Americans raised and hunted their own food or purchased it from local farmers, either directly or through stores in nearby communities. The variety of food was limited, too. Whereas today's grocery store customers can browse through row after row of brightly packaged food items, through the mid-nineteenth century the majority of Americans sustained themselves on a limited menu of wild game, vegetables, wheat and other grains, and the meat and other assorted by-products of domesticated livestock (such as milk, eggs, and butter).

Since American families knew where their food was coming from—and since they relied primarily on natural resources like grass, soil, sunshine, and water to create that food—they saw no need for government oversight of that part of their lives. As America's villages, towns, and cities expanded, though, the merchants, farmers, butchers, and fishers who controlled the food supply became less familiar to customers. In some cases food providers took advantage of this anonymity to engage in dishonest business practices. Some merchants falsified the weight or volume of the foods they sold. Others diluted their products with cheap filler material in order to make more money. Unscrupulous bakers, for example, sometimes added chalk to their bread, while sellers of wine stretched their supply by adding water. This process of adding inferior, impure, or unnecessary ingredients came to be known as adulteration. By the late eighteenth century several laws forbidding the practice had been passed by local authorities or state legislatures.

Regulation of the U.S. food supply took another leap forward in the late nineteenth century. Scientists, physicians, and public health officials around the world made a number of important discoveries about the role that bacteria, viruses, and other microscopic germs play in causing illness. Armed with this knowledge, American cities and states began passing laws designed to reduce their citizens' vulnerability to fearsome disease-carrying germs—also known as pathogens—lurking in their food and water supplies. They passed laws to protect drinking water from sewage contamination and launched programs to teach people about the importance of hand washing and other hygienic practices.

Another important food safety development was the pasteurization of milk. Pasteurization was a revolutionary process invented by French scientist Louis Pasteur. It killed pathogens in raw milk that carried typhoid fever, scarlet fever, diphtheria, tuberculosis, and other dreaded diseases. Although people were slow to recognize pasteurization's health benefits, by the 1920s pasteurization programs came into widespread use across the United States. Pasteurization greatly reduced deaths and illnesses from contaminated milk, and it remains standard practice today.

Slaughterhouse Horrors Spur New Regulations

Despite the introduction of pasteurization and the rise of state food adulteration laws, regulations governing the preparation and sale of food remained modest in size and scope at the dawn of the twentieth century. In 1906, however, author Upton Sinclair published a book that dramatically changed American attitudes about the need for additional food regulation. *The Jungle* was a novel set in Chicago, which was the center of the nation's meatpacking industry at the turn of the century. The meatpacking workers who populated Sinclair's book were fictional, but the conditions he described in the city's stockyards and slaughterhouses—factories where cows, hogs, and other animals were killed and converted into beef and pork products—were all too real. *The Jungle* depicted a world of appalling filth and disease, and it bluntly warned that American families were being fed a steady diet of spoiled and contaminated meat.

Sinclair's book sparked a tremendous public uproar from horrified readers, and a shaken Congress acted promptly to quench their outrage. By the end of 1906 two major federal food safety bills had been crafted, passed, and signed into law by President Theodore Roosevelt. The first of these laws was the Pure Food and Drug Act. This legislation banned the transport or sale of mislabeled or adulterated food, drinks, and drugs across state lines. It also gave the U.S. Department

Deplorable conditions for animals and workers are depicted in an illustration of a slaughterhouse in Chicago, Illinois, in the 1880s. The publication of The Jungle *in 1906 brought public attention to the filth and disease found in America's meatpacking industry and prompted increased food safety regulations.*

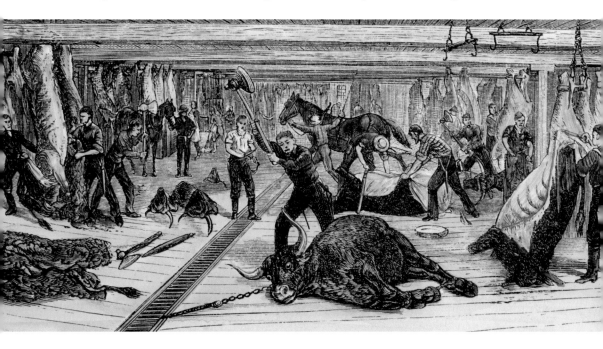

of Agriculture's Bureau of Chemistry (known today as the Food and Drug Administration or FDA) the authority to inspect meat products and slaughterhouse operations.

The other major law that owed its existence to public outrage over *The Jungle* was the 1906 Meat Inspection Act. This legislation replaced a much weaker meat inspection law that had been passed in 1890. The new law ordered the U.S. Department of Agriculture (USDA) to conduct regular inspections of slaughterhouses and meatpacking plants to make sure they followed sanitary standards and used only healthy livestock. These visual and manual inspections were not sophisticated enough to detect the presence of disease-carrying bacteria in animals or meat products. They did succeed, however, in weeding out obviously sick animals and spoiled meat that meatpackers had once offered for sale to unsuspecting customers. As the quality of beef, pork, and lamb improved, rates of disease from meat-borne infections steadily declined across the United States.

Tragedy Sparks Passage of More Safety Regulations

Federal regulation of food did not change much from the 1910s through the mid-1930s. A few modest food-related laws and rules emerged during these years, but they were primarily concerned with labeling or shoring up narrow pieces of the rapidly expanding food industry. The Seafood Inspection Act of 1934, for example, put new FDA procedures in place for ensuring the freshness of shrimp caught by Gulf Coast shrimpers.

Thirty-one years after the publication of *The Jungle*, however, the American food industry was once again rocked by an event that intensified public concerns about the safety of the nation's food supply. That fall, Americans opened their newspapers and read about an unfolding tragedy that eventually claimed the lives of more than one hundred people in fifteen states. These fatalities were traced to "elixir sulfanilamide," a medicine produced and distributed by a drug manufacturer based in Tennessee.

Elixir sulfanilamide was a liquid form of sulfanilamide, a safe and well-established drug that was commonly prescribed

Upton Sinclair Describes America's Slaughterhouses

In 1906 author Upton Sinclair published *The Jungle,* a novel based on his own observations of Chicago's meat-packing industry. In this excerpt, the author tells readers how early-twentieth-century slaughterhouses took spoiled and disease-ridden pork and repackaged it to sell to an unsuspecting public:

There was never the least attention paid to what was cut up for sausage; there would come all the way back from Europe old sausage that had been rejected, and that was mouldy and white—it would be dosed with borax and glycerine, and dumped into the hoppers, and made over again for home consumption. There would be meat that had tumbled out on the floor, in the dirt and sawdust, where the workers had tramped and spit uncounted billions of consumption [tuberculosis] germs. There would be meat stored in great piles in rooms; and the water from leaky roofs would drop over it, and thousands of rats would race about on it. It was too dark in these storage places to see well, but a man could run his hand over these piles of meat and sweep off handfuls of the dried dung of rats. These rats were nuisances, and the packers would put poisoned bread out for them; they would die, and then rats, bread, and meat would go into the hoppers together. This is no fairy story and no joke. . . . There were things that went into the sausage in comparison with which a poisoned rat was a tidbit.

Upton Sinclair. *The Jungle.* New York: Doubleday, Page, 1906, pp. 161–162.

by physicians to treat streptococcal infections. Prior to 1937, the drug had only been available in tablet or powder form, but a Tennessee drugmaker decided that a liquid version might be even more popular. The company's chief chemist discovered that by adding a chemical known as diethylene glycol, he could dissolve sulfanilamide into liquid form. The company laboratory then added some raspberry flavoring and sent more than 600 shipments of the liquid medicine to pharmacies and physicians across the country. The safety of the new drug compound was never tested, however. When doctors began prescribing it to patients, deaths began to mount. Investigators later determined that the diethylene glycol additive was a toxic substance similar to antifreeze.

The mass poisoning prompted outpourings of fury and grief from the American public—and from doctors as well. One physician wrote that six of his patients, including his best friend, were killed after "they took medicine that I prescribed for them innocently . . . [not knowing that it] had become a deadly poison in its newest and most modern form. . . . That realization has given me such days and nights of mental and spiritual agony as I did not believe a human being could undergo and survive."[1]

In the wake of this awful tragedy, Congress responded with the Food, Drug, and Cosmetic Act (FDCA) of 1938, which placed strong new regulations on the operations of drug companies. The pharmaceutical industry, though, was not the only industry to be affected by this law. Numerous provisions of the FDCA were squarely aimed at the food industry, which had outgrown many of the safety regulations that had been crafted at the beginning of the century. The FDCA authorized the federal government to beef up its inspections of food manufacturing and processing plants. It also gave the FDA new powers to monitor the care and treatment of livestock, set safety standards for infant formula, and strengthen food labeling requirements. Finally, the law declared that food products could be classified as "adulterated"—and thus illegal—if they contained potentially dangerous chemicals.

The World's Breadbasket

At the same time that the U.S. government expanded its oversight of the food industry, American agriculture grew at an amazing rate. Boosted by new farming machines, improvements in ocean shipping, and innovations in refrigeration and other food preservation technologies, American farmers and ranchers were able to deliver their products to hungry towns and cities all across the United States—and even around the world. By the early 1900s, in fact, U.S. exports of meat and grains had become so great that Americans were proudly describing their nation as the breadbasket of the world.

This decades-long run of agricultural expansion and prosperity came to a shattering stop with the arrival of the Great Depression in the early 1930s. The Great Depression was a terrible economic crisis that produced record levels of business closings, bank failures, and unemployment in America and around the world. It was made even worse by the so-called Dust Bowl, in which several farm states in the Great Plains region lost millions of acres of farmland to drought and dust storms in the mid-1930s. When journalist Ernie Pyle toured the Dust Bowl, he reported that in many regions "there was not a tree or a blade of grass, or a dog or a cow or a human being—nothing whatsoever, nothing at all but gray raw earth and a few farmhouses and barns, sticking up from the dark gray sea like white cattle skeletons on the desert. . . . [It was] the saddest land I have ever seen."[2]

President Franklin D. Roosevelt responded to the Great Depression with a wave of new laws and programs known collectively as the New Deal. Several New Deal policies were crafted, as author Michael Pollan notes, "to rescue farmers from the disastrous effects of growing too much food—far more than Americans could afford to buy."[3] This oversupply of food was keeping crop, dairy, and livestock prices so low that farmers could not survive. The U.S. government decided to address this problem by paying farmers to slaughter huge numbers of livestock and buying up excess corn and other crops for storage. In addition, the government began paying some farmers *not* to grow crops. These payments served to keep supplies of wheat, corn, and other crops from rising to a point where they would cause a crash in crop prices.

FOOD FACT

Americans make up about 5 percent of the world's population but account for more than 15 percent of the world's total meat consumption.

Farming Becomes Big Business

An aerial shot shows an expansive patchwork of farm crops as far as the eye can see in Northern California. Farming became big business in the United States in the decades following World War II.

When America's economy pulled out of the Depression after World War II, the reforms implemented by Roosevelt took full effect. Since farmers were now better protected from the threat of low crop prices, they could get bigger and bigger without fear of financial ruin. Small farmers, though, had difficulty keeping up in this environment, which rewarded big operations that could afford all the fancy new pesticides, fertilizers, mechanical milking machines, and tractors that were coming on the market. By the close of the 1950s, almost 50 percent of all U.S. farmland was owned by less than 4 percent of the nation's farmers.

The push toward "mega farms" further intensified in the 1970s, when the federal government replaced New Deal farm policies with a system that encouraged farmers to plant "from fence row to fence row"[4] and to use herbicides, pesticides, fertilizers, and anything else that would boost their yields of corn, wheat, soybeans, apples, and other commodities. Producers of beef, pork, and other meat products got the same message.

Supporters of these new policies believed that increasing America's food supply would make prices go down in butcher shops and grocery stores around the country. They were right—food prices did drop. But the new system made it harder for family farms to survive unless they concentrated on growing one or two of the most valuable commodity crops—usually corn, wheat, or soybeans. Big farming corporations, on the other hand, thrived in this environment. Armed with lots of money, they invested heavily in new machines, new irrigation technologies, and the latest fertilizers, herbicides, and pesticides.

New Methods for Raising Crops and Livestock

Farmers also began buying up crop seeds that had undergone genetic changes by scientists to increase the size and growing capacity of crops. Commercial use of these genetically modified (GM) seeds (also known as transgenic or bioengineered seeds) soared after 1992, when the FDA formally approved their use. Two years later, the first commercial GM food product—the Flavr Savr tomato—was shipped to American grocery stores. The push toward GM seeds intensified even more after that, especially since easily modifiable crops like corn and soybeans are used as ingredients in so many different processed foods. By 2011 88 percent of corn and 93 percent of the soybeans planted in the United States were genetically modified, according to the U.S. Department of Agriculture.

Producers of beef, pork, poultry, and dairy products also became steadily more dependent on scientific advances in agriculture. Most notably, they dramatically expanded their

Thousands of chickens crowd in an egg-producing facility in Oklahoma in 2003. Critics charge that factory farms create an environmental hazard and disregard animal welfare.

use of growth hormones and other government-approved chemicals that increased the size of their chickens, cows, and hogs. Use of antibiotics—disease-fighting medicines—also surged in the meat industry during the 1970s and 1980s. The increased reliance on antibiotics stemmed from the fact that cows, chickens, and other animals were increasingly kept in crowded warehouses, where they could be raised and slaughtered cheaply. Since large numbers of animals confined in such close quarters were at greater risk of spreading disease, heavy applications of antibiotics became a fast and inexpensive way for feedlot operators to reduce the risk of a disease outbreak.

Within the food industry these massive facilities were called Industrial Animal Feeding Operations (IAFOs) or Concentrated Animal Feeding Operations (CAFOs). Among critics, however, CAFOs were known as "factory farms," and during the 1980s and 1990s environmental protection groups and consumer advocacy organizations condemned them on several fronts. Opponents of factory farms charged that the huge volumes of animal waste generated in CAFOs posed a pollution threat to area rivers, lakes, and underground water supplies. They also said that these operations treated animals inhumanely. Finally, critics expressed alarm about the heavy volume of antibiotics that were being introduced into America's chickens, cows, and pigs in these operations. They warned that excessive reliance on antibiotics might eventually create frightening new antibiotic-resistant strains of pathogens that could sicken or even kill humans if they entered the food supply.

A New Wave of Food Safety Laws

Local and state lawmakers and agencies frantically tried to keep pace with the rapid industrialization of the food industry. They crafted new policies and laws to better ensure that farmers, livestock operations, and big food-processing companies were marketing their products honestly, raising their crops and animals responsibly, and producing food that was safe to eat. Several states, for example, passed laws that either prohibited the establishment of new factory farms or imposed new environmental and public health restrictions on their operations.

New food regulations also were introduced at the national level to better protect consumers. The 1990 Nutrition Labeling and Education Act required all packaged foods to contain standardized information on their nutritional content. It was followed six years later by the Food Quality Protection Act (FQPA). This law gave the U.S. Environmental Protection Agency (EPA) new powers to impose new safety standards for pesticide use. "If a pesticide poses a danger to our children, then it won't be in our food," declared President Bill Clinton when he signed the act into law. "I like to think of it as the 'peace of mind act,' because it will give parents the peace of mind that comes from knowing that the fruits, the vegetables, the grains that they put down in front of their children are safe."[5]

Other food safety laws followed as well. In 2004, for example, Congress passed the Food Allergen Labeling and Consumer Protection Act (FALCPA). This law required manufacturers to clearly label packaged foods that contained any ingredients from the eight major food groups that account for most food allergies.

Despite this parade of new laws, however, the safety of America's food supply remained in question. Although fed-

Nutrition labels are required by law on all packaged foods in the United States. In order to further inform consumers, food manufacturers must also identify ingredients that are potential allergens.

eral health regulations had been shored up to better protect consumers from fraudulent advertising and toxic additives and pesticides, they remained silent when it came to dangerous food-borne bacteria such as salmonella, listeria, campylobacter, and *Escherichia coli*, better known as *E. coli*.

Link Between Food-Borne Pathogens and Mass Production

Until the 1970s and 1980s, most of these nasty pathogens were not even present in the human food chain—or if they were, they existed in only mild forms. Food safety experts and scientists believe, however, that modern food production techniques opened the door for these bacteria to enter the food supply. "More and more animals are raised on a single farm, so hundreds of thousands of pigs, or hundreds of thousands of chickens, may be raised under one roof. This gives the opportunity for pathogens to spread from one animal to another," states Dr. Robert Tauxe, chief of the food-borne illness division at the U.S. Centers for Disease Control and Prevention (CDC).

> And when they are transported to slaughter, animals from many different farms may go in the same truck or the same transport freight to the slaughterhouse. Again, there's the opportunity for the exchange of these bacteria. As the line speeds and the general efficiency of the slaughter plants increase, there may also be a greater opportunity for contamination to spread from one carcass to another. I suspect that the industrialization of our meat supply opened up a conduit for . . . infections to pass through to the consumer.[6]

Experts also emphasize that once food has been tainted with harmful pathogens—usually by direct contact with infected animals' waste or stomach contents during slaughtering or processing—outbreaks are very difficult to contain. Today's hamburger—whether packaged in grocery stores or in patty form for use by fast-food restaurants—routinely contains meat trimmings from dozens or even hundreds of different cows. If even one of those cows carried *E. coli* or salmonella, then thousands of pounds of hamburger are at risk of contamination. "The meatpacking system that arose to supply the nation's fast food chains—an industry molded to serve their needs, to provide massive amounts of uniform ground beef so that all of McDonald's hamburgers would taste the same—has proved to be an extremely efficient system for spreading disease,"[7] wrote investigative journalist Eric Schlosser.

Finally, the potential for outbreaks of food-borne illness has risen due to the sophistication of America's transportation system. "High-speed distribution means contaminated food can be in consumers' homes, and stomachs, long before the contamination is detected," explains environmental journalist Paul Roberts. "The very innovations that let us feed so many so well can also nourish an epidemic—and ensure that its impacts will be devastating."[8]

Outbreaks Revive Fears About Food Safety

The first major outbreaks of food-borne pathogens in the United States occurred in the mid-1980s. In 1985 salmonella-tainted milk killed two people and sickened another 150,000 people in the Chicago metropolitan area. That same year in Southern California, an outbreak of listeria in soft cheese claimed forty-eight lives, including nineteen stillbirths and ten infants. Another 1985 listeria outbreak—this one due to contaminated milk—caused more than 16,000 confirmed cases of food poisoning in Illinois and surrounding Midwest states.

These outbreaks were greatly alarming to farmers, scientists, and public health officials, in part because pathogen-infected livestock did not show any outward symptoms. Contaminated cattle looked and behaved just the same as ones that were not carrying the pathogens. "We had always believed that if you kept the livestock from getting sick, the food was safe," said Lester Crawford, who worked in the USDA's meat inspection department and later served a three-year stint as chief of the FDA. "The phrase we used was 'healthy livestock, healthy people.' But here was a case where livestock were thriving and people were getting not just sick, but *violently* sick."[9]

Grappling with Mad Cow Disease

In 1986 British public health authorities identified a frightening new and fatal brain disease that was spreading across that nation's cattle population. Dubbed "mad cow disease" because infected animals appeared aggressive and disoriented, the disease was officially called bovine spongiform encephalopathy (BSE). The discovery of BSE was enormously damaging to the British beef industry, which had to destroy huge numbers of cattle in an effort to stop the outbreak.

In 1996 investigators documented that humans who ate BSE-infected meat could actually contract a deadly form of the disease. The knowledge that mad cow disease was capable of jumping the species barrier from cattle to humans prompted the United States government to impose a wide range of new anti-BSE regulations, including bans on certain cattle feeds linked to the disease and bans on the processing of "downer" cows (animals too sick to stand or walk) for food. As of 2011 U.S. public health authorities have identified three cases of mad cow disease in America. The most recent of these came in 2006, when officials determined that a cow in Alabama was suffering from the disease.

Cows feed at a ranch in Mabton, Washington, that was quarantined in 2003 after being traced to a case of mad cow disease.

Reports of food poisoning from pathogens increased steadily through the late 1980s and early 1990s, but it was not until late 1992 that another major outbreak garnered national headlines. In December doctors in the Seattle area observed a sudden surge in emergency room visits from children suffering from bloody diarrhea and rare kidney problems. Investigators eventually traced the problem to undercooked hamburgers from the Jack in the Box fast food chain. These hamburgers, which were laced with *E. coli* bacteria, killed four children and sickened more than seven hundred people up and down the West Coast before the outbreak was contained in February 1993.

The stories of the children who died from the Jack in the Box outbreak elicited an outpouring of grief and outrage. Five-year-old Lauren Rudolph's parents had taken her to a San Diego–area Jack in the Box just before Christmas as a reward for getting good grades on her report card. Within two days, she was bedridden with horrible nausea and diarrhea. By Christmas Eve she had been admitted to a local hospital, but her condition worsened despite increasingly frantic treatment from doctors and nurses. On Christmas Day Lauren suffered a massive heart attack and fell into a coma. Three days later the first-grader was dead, a victim of *E. coli* bacteria. Author Nicols Fox notes that "no one at the hospital had thought to run the standard tests for [E. coli] while Lauren was alive. If they had . . . the future for more than seven hundred other people might have been different."[10]

Tragedy Prompts New Meat Safety Regulations

After the Jack in the Box outbreak, American consumers demanded action from their government. The USDA responded to the Jack in the Box crisis by imposing significant new safety regulations. For the first time, it classified a bacteria—*E. coli*—as an adulterant. This new classification meant that the meat industry would have to take the same anti-contamination measures against the pathogen that it already did against human-made toxins. It also approved a

new meat safety monitoring system called Hazard Analysis and Critical Control Point (HACCP).

Under HACCP regulations, meat processing companies were forced to improve their food safety procedures and invest in new food safety technologies. Testing of food quality at various points in processing operations became routine. Companies also discovered that if they failed to meet federal safety standards for pathogens, the USDA had the power to pull its inspectors out of their facilities. If no inspectors were present, then the company could not obtain an "inspected and passed by USDA" stamp for its products. Since these stamps were required by grocery stores, food companies had to police themselves if they wanted to keep the inspectors working.

The introduction of HACCP undoubtedly improved meat quality and safety. As time passed, though, some consumer

A microbiologist at a meat-processing plant inspects a bacteria culture as part of a routine quality control check. A deadly E. coli outbreak in the early 1990s prompted regulations forcing meat processors to improve their safety procedures.

advocates and USDA food safety regulators complained that the system, which made food companies responsible for carrying out HACCP programs, still did not provide enough food production safeguards. They charged that food makers still sometimes ignored safety regulations if the regulations reduced financial profitability. When companies are permitted to take on food safety responsibilities without sufficient government oversight, summarized one former USDA meat inspector, "it's like the wolf guarding the henhouse."[11]

Growing Pressure on Congress to Act

The new safety regulations failed to protect the United States from another wave of disease outbreaks caused by foodborne pathogens. In 1994 salmonella-tainted ice cream sickened at least 740 people in thirty states (officials suspect that the number of food poisoning cases from this incident was actually far higher). Two years later, an *E. coli* outbreak that sickened sixty people was traced to premixed lettuce packages. In 1998 listeria-laced deli meats and hot dogs that had been produced at a Pennsylvania food-processing plant were linked to twenty-one deaths and more than a hundred illnesses in almost two dozen states.

By the close of the 1990s, growing numbers of American consumers were expressing mounting concern—and sometimes outright alarm—about whether the food they were feeding their families was safe. These worries further intensified in the new century with a flurry of additional outbreaks. In 2000 sixty-five people were sickened and a three-year-old girl died when two Milwaukee-area restaurants served up undercooked beef infected with *E. coli*. One year later, the United States endured 163 recalls of contaminated meat that totaled over 100 million pounds. In 2003, green onions that had been imported from Mexico and used at a Chi-Chi's Mexican Restaurant in Pennsylvania sickened more than six hundred customers and killed four people. Investigators later found that the onions were infected with the hepatitis A virus. In the summer of 2006 America was rocked by an outbreak of *E. coli* from contaminated spinach. Investigators believe that the spinach became infected from irrigation water that

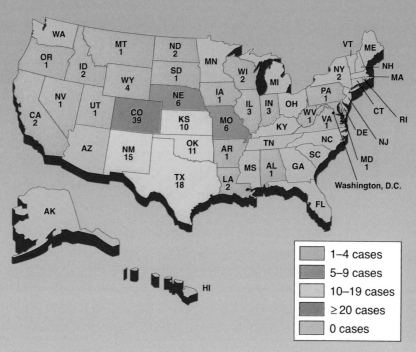

The Spread of a 2011 Listeria Outbreak

Legend:
- 1–4 cases
- 5–9 cases
- 10–19 cases
- ≥ 20 cases
- 0 cases

Note: In September 2011 public health officials discovered that cantaloupe raised at a farm in Colorado was contaminated with listeria. Within two months the outbreak had spread to twenty-eight states.

Taken from: www.cdc.gov/listeria/outbreaks/cantaloupes-jensen-farms/110211/map.html.

was contaminated with cattle feces. By the time the outbreak was contained, three people were dead and nearly two hundred more had been sickened. In 2008 a salmonella outbreak in processed peanut butter killed nine people and sickened at least twenty-two thousand others. Two years later, more than nineteen hundred illnesses from salmonella were traced to two egg farms in Iowa, prompting a recall of 500 million eggs across more than a dozen states. In 2011 listeria-laced cantaloupe from Colorado claimed the lives of twenty-five people scattered across twelve states (people were sickened in a total of twenty-eight states).

The FDA Food Safety Modernization Act

For many years American agribusiness—a term that encompasses all of the various sectors of the food industry—was able to use its political influence to stop many suggested reforms. Even after the 1992–1993 Jack in the Box outbreak convinced U.S. authorities to take new steps to combat *E. coli,* the meat industry managed to fend off calls for regulations that would target other food-borne bacteria, such as salmonella and listeria.

Food safety advocates did not give up, though. They continued to press for additional regulation, and in 2010 Congress passed the biggest overhaul of America's food-safety laws since the 1930s. The bill, officially known as the FDA Food Safety Modernization Act, was signed into law by President Barack Obama on January 4, 2011. The law affects all whole and processed foods except meat, poultry, and some egg products, all of which are regulated by the U.S. Department of Agriculture. The Food Safety Modernization Act requires the food industry to make new investments in bacteria-fighting technology and gives the FDA full authority to recall tainted food, increase inspections of farms and food-processing facilities, and create a food-tracking system that will allow authorities to quickly identify the source of outbreaks from food-borne pathogens.

Some supporters of the law worried that congressional opponents might seek to torpedo these reforms by withholding funding for the new programs. Other advocates, however, voiced confidence that America had taken a major step forward in improving the quality and safety of its food supply. "This is a big victory for consumers that finally brings food-safety laws into the 21st century," proclaimed Jean Halloran of Consumers Union. "This win is a powerful testament to the people across the country who came to Washington to tell their lawmakers how contaminated food had killed their loved ones or left them horribly sick. This win is for them and all Americans."[12]

CHAPTER 2

The Guardians of Food Safety in America

Many local, state, and federal agencies share responsibility for protecting America's food supply. This governmental network, though, is not the sole voice on the nation's food safety issues. Public health advocates, research scientists, environmental groups, agribusiness, and farmers all contribute to policy decisions about the size, shape, and extent of U.S. food and drink regulations.

Local Responsibilities in Food Safety

Local and state agencies carry out a wide range of duties to monitor food safety in their communities. Their exact responsibilities vary from town to town, county to county, and state to state, but in general they act as the first line of defense against food-borne disease outbreaks, contamination of food and water supplies from industrial toxins, and other threats. Local agencies and inspectors, in fact, carry out the great majority of food safety inspections that take place in the United States every year. "[Local] inspectors routinely look for sanitation problems, temperature problems with refrigerated or stored foods, and employee sanitation concerns, such as personal hygiene among food handlers," writes scholar James T. O'Reilly. "Closing filthy restaurant

A food inspector reviews conditions at a restaurant in Nebraska. State and local agencies dedicate a range of resources to monitoring food safety.

kitchens or ordering destruction of a truckload of defrosted meat in a broken trailer does not get headline news coverage, but this phase of real consumer protection is vitally important."[13]

Funding and political support varies wildly for the estimated three thousand local public health agencies that are involved in food safety issues affecting their communities. Some local agencies benefit from steady administrative leadership, generous and reliable funding, and strong community support. Other agencies take a less active role, either because of inadequate funding or hostility from local politicians and businesses. In general, however, local health departments and food inspection agencies have the following food safety responsibilities:

- Collecting and responding to local food-safety related consumer complaints.
- Performing laboratory tests on potentially contaminated food and food sources.
- Responding to local outbreaks of food-borne illness.
- Licensing and inspecting food safety standards at local grocery stores, restaurants, and other establishments that sell food and drinks.
- Providing technical training and education on food safety issues.

State Responsibilities in Food Safety

State-level public health, environmental, and consumer protection agencies also provide a variety of food safety functions. They often undertake these responsibilities in cooperation with—and under the guidance of—federal food safety agencies. For example, more than 80 percent of the inspections of meat and poultry processing operations across the United States are actually carried out by state agencies. These inspections, however, are conducted on behalf of the U.S. Department of Agriculture, which sets the food safety standards that the businesses must meet.

- States are generally responsible for carrying out the following food safety functions:
- Carrying out recalls of food and drink products that are found to pose a threat to public health.
- Monitoring for outbreaks of food-borne illness at all stages of food production, from the farm to the dinner table.
- Performing laboratory tests to identify food-related pathogens.
- Setting standards for cleanliness and safe treatment of food products in grocery stores and restaurants; some state agencies also carry out inspections of these facilities.

- Inspecting farming operations to check on animal health and enforce restrictions on the use of pesticides and herbicides.
- Providing technical training and education on food safety issues.

Food Safety Responsibilities of the Food and Drug Administration

At the national level, responsibility for food safety is divided among four federal agencies. The best known of these agencies is probably the U.S. Food and Drug Administration (FDA), which is part of the U.S. Department of Health and Human Services (HHS). In addition to overseeing the safety and security of drugs, medical devices, and cosmetics, the FDA is charged with ensuring that most foods and beverages in the United States—including those that come from overseas—are accurately labeled and safe to eat and drink. To that end, the agency sets broad operating and safety standards from farm to table for about 80 percent of the foods and drinks bought and consumed by Americans.

The FDA's main food safety division is the Center for Food Safety and Applied Nutrition (CFSAN). Products regulated by CFSAN include fruits and vegetables, dairy products, seafood, exotic meats, and all processed foods. The only foods that are not regulated by CFSAN are beef, pork, poultry, and other domesticated meat products. Regulation of these products is the responsibility of the U.S. Department of Agriculture (USDA). The FDA and the USDA share responsibility for ensuring the safety of eggs. Finally, the FDA's Center for Veterinary Medicine (CVM) oversees the safety of animal feeds and drugs, including those used in the raising of pigs, cows, and other food-producing animals.

Despite the fact that the FDA is responsible for the safety of 80 percent of the U.S. food supply, it receives only

FOOD FACT

Due to funding shortfalls, FDA inspections of America's food supply declined by 81 percent between 1972 and 2007, according to the Center for Science in the Public Interest.

An FDA field inspector prepares samples of imported food for laboratory analysis. The FDA works to ensure that most food and beverages in the U.S. market, including those from other countries, are safe and properly labeled.

about 40 percent of the federal government dollars devoted to food safety; most of the rest goes to the USDA. In 2010 the Food and Drug Administration maintained a force of more than nineteen hundred inspectors in field offices throughout the United States, as well as nine hundred employees in its Washington, D.C., headquarters. According to the Congressional Research Service, these employees are responsible for overseeing the operations of more than forty-four thousand domestic food manufacturers, one hundred thousand grain elevators, food warehouses, and other facilities, and two hundred thousand foreign food facilities.

Due to budget shortfalls, the FDA has been unable to inspect these various facilities as frequently as it would like. FDA officials estimate that surprise inspections of U.S. food manufacturers only take place every five to ten years. They hasten to add, though, that "high-risk" facilities—those that have a record of food safety violations—are inspected much more frequently. Altogether, the HHS reports that less than 30 percent of domestic food manufacturing facilities are inspected by the FDA each year. The impact of the 2011 FDA Food Safety Modernization Act on the agency's inspection rates is not yet known. The legislation increases the FDA's food safety authority and gives the agency new responsibilities, but it is an open question whether future Congresses will provide it with the money it needs to hire new inspectors and conduct new tests.

Researching Food-Borne Illness at the Centers for Disease Control and Prevention

The HHS is also home to a second federal agency with critical food safety and security responsibilities. The Centers for Disease Control and Prevention (CDC) is the chief scientific investigator on food-borne illnesses in the United States. It works closely with local and state public health departments to identify and control food-borne pathogens responsible for outbreaks of disease. CDC laboratories also carry out ongoing research into ways that food and beverage safety can be enhanced at all stages of production.

Over the years CDC has established several food-borne illness surveillance programs. The most prominent of these programs is FoodNet. First launched in 1995 in partnership with the USDA, FoodNet collects data on food-borne illness outbreaks across the United States. It includes research studies, physician and population surveys, and ongoing monitoring of microbiology laboratories that conduct tests on disease outbreaks. "FoodNet data," summarizes the Congressional Research Service, "allows CDC to have a clearer picture of the incidence and causes of foodborne illness and to establish baseline data against which to measure the success of changes in food safety programs."[14]

A Mosquito-Swatting Agency

The Centers for Disease Control and Prevention (CDC) is known today as America's leading research agency dedicated to disease prevention. It stands at the forefront of national and global efforts to prevent and control infectious and chronic diseases and environmental threats to individual and community health. When the agency was first established in 1946 as the Communicable Disease Center, however, it focused primarily on malaria, an infectious disease spread by mosquitoes. CDC administrators thus launched a sustained war against America's mosquito population. The agency's focus on mosquitoes was so great, in fact, that an early CDC organization chart was drawn in the shape of a mosquito.

The main way that CDC carried out its war against mosquitoes was through massive sprayings of DDT, a strong chemical insecticide. DDT spraying campaigns dramatically reduced mosquito populations in many communities, and malaria cases plummeted across the country. Beginning in the early 1960s, though, Rachel Carson and other scientists warned that DDT and other synthetic pesticides and herbicides posed a growing threat to wildlife and natural ecosystems. They also expressed concern about the possible long-term effects of these chemicals on human health. Research studies documenting the dangers of DDT proliferated throughout the 1960s. They showed that the chemical contributed to the risk of cancer and the decline of populations of eagles and other species. In 1972 the United States banned DDT.

An airplane sprays DDT over a mosquito-infested swamp in Savannah, Georgia, in the 1950s.

Another important CDC program is PulseNet, which acts as an early warning system for outbreaks of food-borne disease. The PulseNet program uses scientific "fingerprinting" of food-borne pathogens to alert state public health laboratories and officials when an outbreak has been detected. The CDC also maintains Epi-X, an Internet-based communication tool that allows CDC officials and state and local public health agencies to access and share information on food-borne illnesses. OutbreakNet is another web-based program that helps the CDC and local, state, and federal agencies cooperate with one another when investigating disease outbreaks due to food-borne bacteria as well as other causes.

The USDA Urges Consumers to "Fight BAC" Against Food-Borne Illness

Keep Food Safe from Bacteria

Clean
Wash hands and surfaces often.

Separate
Don't cross-contaminate.

BAC

Chill
Refrigerate promptly.

Cook
Cook to proper temperatures.

The USDA's Food Safety and Inspection Service

The U.S. Department of Agriculture is responsible for ensuring the safety of virtually all of the meat and poultry products that are consumed in American kitchens, cafeterias, food stands, and restaurants every day. In addition to its inspections and enforcement actions, however, the USDA also has served a historical function as a vocal supporter of the agriculture industry. The USDA's role as a marketing arm for U.S. farmers has undoubtedly helped American agriculture to grow and prosper. This cheerleading function, however, has also led critics to charge that the agency is "an apologist for bad decisions made by the food conglomerates" and "tailors its rules to satisfy industry more than to satisfy the needs of the taxpaying public."[15]

The USDA carries out most of its food safety duties through the Food Safety and Inspection Service (FSIS), which maintained a staff of about ninety-four hundred people in 2010. About eight thousand of these staff members are stationed at one of roughly sixty-three hundred plants across the United States that engage in meat slaughtering and/or processing. FSIS personnel are responsible for continuously monitoring whether these plants are meeting federal safety and sanitary standards. Some states choose to operate their own meat and/or poultry inspection programs. Even in these cases, however, the FSIS is responsible for overseeing the state programs to make sure that they are at least equal to the federal program.

Finally, the FSIS is responsible for certifying that imported meat and poultry products are safe for human consumption. Imported products that fall under the FSIS's responsibility range from popular meats derived from cows, hogs, and chickens to more unusual meat products culled from goats, geese, ostriches, quail, and guinea fowl.

FOOD FACT

The Environmental Protection Agency's regulation of pesticides extends to flea and tick products used by millions of American families each year. The agency monitors these products to protect pets as well as young children from any adverse health effects from their use.

USDA inspectors work at a Nebraska meat processing plant to ensure the facility is meeting federal safety and sanitary standards.

In addition to the FSIS, the USDA includes several other agencies that play a role in protecting the nation's food supply. The Agricultural Research Service (ARS) performs food safety research that the FSIS incorporates into its inspection duties, while the Animal and Plant Health Inspection Service (APHIS) works to protect livestock and crops from diseases and insects. The USDA's Food and Nutrition Service (FNS), meanwhile, coordinates efforts to make sure that school lunch programs are safe and nutritious for children.

Food Safety Responsibilities in Other Parts of the Federal Government

Although the FDA and USDA act as the primary defenders of America's food supply at the federal level, a few other federal agencies also provide food security services at one point or another in the food supply chain. The best known of these agencies is the Environmental Protection Agency (EPA). The

EPA's Office of Prevention, Pesticides, and Toxic Substances establishes legal tolerances or limits on the amount of pesticides that can be safely used on food crops.

The Federal Trade Commission (FTC) is usually associated with consumer protection against unfair business

In 2010 the Federal Trade Commission targeted the makers of POM Wonderful pomegranate juice for making unsubstantiated and misleading health claims about the product.

practices, not food safety. As part of that larger mission, though, the FTC does enforce laws that forbid food companies from making deceptive or untrue statements about their products. The National Marine Fisheries Service, meanwhile, offers voluntary seafood inspection programs to the fisheries industry.

Finally, the Bureau of Alcohol, Tobacco, Firearms, and Explosives (ATF) is responsible for enforcing laws and regulations pertaining to the manufacture, distribution, and use of alcoholic beverages. These regulations include extensive production and distribution guidelines to ensure the safety of beer, wine, and liquor.

The Role of Congress in Food Safety Regulation

Numerous agencies within the federal government share responsibility for ensuring food security and safety in the United States. But the laws that give these agencies their authority are made by the U.S. Congress. In addition, Congress determines how much funding they receive to carry out their missions. Congress thus plays an enormous role in shaping food regulation and safety in the United States.

Any member of Congress, whether serving in the U.S. Senate or the U.S. House of Representatives, is free to introduce proposals for new laws governing food safety or any other policy area. After a bill has been introduced, it is assigned to a committee for review. In the House of Representatives, food safety bills go to one of the following committees for consideration: Agriculture; Energy and Commerce; Oversight and Government Reform; and Science. In the Senate, food safety policy is overseen by the Committee on Agriculture, Nutrition, Forestry; the Committee on Health, Education, Labor, and Pensions; and the Committee on Homeland Security and Governmental Affairs. Historically, congressional committees devoted to food safety issues have been dominated by lawmakers from farm states—states that are heavily reliant on agriculture for their economic prosperity.

The Department of Agriculture's Historic 4-H Program

For millions of American children and teenagers, their most meaningful association with the U.S. Department of Agriculture comes through the agency's respected 4-H program. This youth organization, which is administered by the USDA's National Institute of Food and Agriculture, has over 6 million members in the United States. First established in 1902, the 4-H program focused for many years on the nation's farming families. It became firmly associated in the minds of millions of children with county fairs, state fairs, and other events that celebrate America's agricultural heritage.

Over the years, though, 4-H has developed programs that serve sub-urban and inner-city youth as well as those who live in farming and ranching communities. Some of these programs challenge 4-H youth to increase their skills in science, engineering, mathematics, animal science, and other subjects. Others encourage youngsters to learn about important issues like climate change and global food shortages. One of 4-H's most successful initiatives is its Food Safety and Quality Assurance (FSQA) program. This program helps youth understand their role in producing safe and healthy food—and helps them understand the importance of making wise and ethical decisions related to food production.

A girl shows her 4-H pig at a county fair.

Only if a bill is approved by the assigned committee can it go on for a vote in the full House or Senate. If a mutually satisfactory version passes both houses of Congress, it then goes to the president of the United States for his signature to become law.

CHAPTER 3

The Food-Borne Germs That Make Us Sick

Kayla Boner was a healthy teenage girl who lived in Monroe, Iowa, and dreamed of playing college basketball and becoming a pediatrician. "Kayla was a typical teenager," said her mother, Dana. "She talked on her cell phone too much and argued about her curfew." But she was also a good daughter who willingly helped out with chores and frequently presented fresh flowers to her mom. "They might have been lilacs from the garden, or even just dandelions," recalled Dana, "but she knew how much I liked them."[16]

Kayla celebrated her fourteenth birthday on October 22, 2007. Later on that day, though, she began complaining of a stomachache. Over the next forty-eight hours she developed severe diarrhea, and she was admitted to the local hospital. On October 29 her kidneys shut down. Laboratory tests eventually determined that she was infected with a deadly *E. coli* germ that was attacking her kidneys. Doctors told Kayla and her parents that she almost certainly contracted the infection from contaminated food.

Over the next several days doctors and nurses worked frantically to help Kayla withstand the infection, but her condition steadily worsened. She became disoriented and her blood pressure jumped to frightening levels. In the early morning hours of November 2 she suffered a series of strokes that left her without brain function. Kayla died later that morning after she was taken off the life support machinery that was keeping her breathing. "I had a very healthy child," said Dana. "Ten days later, she was gone."[17] To make matters even worse, authorities were never able to trace the *E. coli* pathogen that claimed Kayla's life back to a particular food product. "If your child is killed by a gun or by a person, we look for a killer—but when it's meat or food poisoning, it's done," said Dana. "You have no answers what happened, why it happened, how could it happen. . . . There's nothing you can do."[18]

The *E. coli* Threat to America's Food Supply

The *E. coli* germ that took Kayla's life is just one of several scary types of toxic bacteria that have been responsible for outbreaks of food-borne illness in the United States and around the world over the past few decades. It is probably the best known of these pathogens, however, since the most virulent strain of the bacteria, known as *E. coli O157:H7*, was the culprit in so many major outbreaks in the 1980s and 1990s.

E. coli bacteria have long been present in cows, other livestock, and humans, but until the early 1980s it was a relatively harmless bug. Although people sometimes ingested meat containing *E. coli,* human stomach acid was usually able to kill off the bacteria before it could do any damage. Beginning in the mid-twentieth century, however, raisers of beef cattle switched their livestock to a diet of corn, which made cow digestive systems more acidic than they had been when the animals were fed grass or hay. The switch gradually made *E. coli* more resistant to acid.

Around this same period, the *E. coli* strain *O157:H7* took on a much more poisonous form when it interacted with a toxic bacterium called *Shigella*. The result, says environmental journalist David Roberts, was a pathogen "that could withstand the acid shock of the human stomach and reach the intestine intact, where the *shiga* toxins could work their deviltry. Precisely when these adaptations occurred isn't known, but by 1982, when an outbreak of *O157:H7* sickened forty-seven McDonald's customers, the bug's new weaponry was both fully formed and more lethal than anything investigators had ever seen."[19]

The *E. coli* germ usually escapes the digestive system of cows and contaminates meat during the slaughtering process. Humans get infections when they digest undercooked beef, although people also can get sick from water, milk, and other foods that have come into contact with *E. coli*–laced meat or animal waste. In addition, *E. coli* bacteria have been known

A wholesale produce dealer inspects bags of spinach that were quarantined during a deadly E. coli *outbreak in 2006.*

to be passed from person to person by contact, especially in crowded places like nursing homes, schools, and day care centers.

Symptoms of *E. coli* usually appear within seven days of infection. They usually include severe abdominal cramps and severe or bloody diarrhea. Nausea or vomiting also are common. In many cases, people recover from an *E. coli* attack after a few days of misery. In severe cases, though, the bacteria turns life-threatening by attacking red blood cells, which in turn can cause kidney failure. This complication, which is known as hemolytic uremic syndrome, is particularly dangerous for children.

Outbreaks of food-borne sickness from *E. coli O157:H7* have declined since 1994, when the U.S. government began classifying that strain as an adulterant. This measure forced the nation's beef industry to test for the presence of *E. coli O157:H7* and take other safety precautions to guard against the bacteria. Nevertheless, the Centers for Disease Control and Prevention estimate that *E. coli O157:H7* still accounts for more than eighty thousand infections and more than twenty-one hundred hospitalizations annually across the United States.

Meanwhile, several other strains of *E. coli* bacteria that were not placed on the government's adulterant list became significant public health threats in their own right during the 1990s and 2000s. By 2010, in fact, the CDC estimated that "non-*O157*" strains of *E. coli* accounted for twice the number of illnesses as *E. coli O157:H7*. In 2011 the U.S. Department of Agriculture finally added six other *E. coli* strains—*O26, O45, O103, O111, O121* and *O145*—to the list of adulterants for which meat processors must test.

Salmonella—America's Deadliest Food-Borne Pathogen

Salmonella is another bacteria that has infiltrated America's food supply. This pathogen, in fact, now ranks as the country's deadliest source of food-borne illness. According to the CDC, food-borne salmonella poisoning strikes 1 million Americans every year. Of these cases, about twenty thousand

Uncertainty in Determining Rates of Food-Borne Illness

Public health authorities and scientific research agencies like the Centers for Disease Control and Prevention work very hard to figure out how often Americans become sick from food-borne pathogens. Researchers admit that determining the exact number of people who are sickened from food-borne microbes is virtually impossible because many cases go unreported. In other instances, people who become sick from contaminated food assume that they are simply suffering from the flu or some other non-food bug.

Nonetheless, food safety researchers have become much more adept at calculating rates of food-borne illness since the late 1970s, when they first began undertaking such studies. Today's scientists use sophisticated surveys, hospital records, and many other data sources to make their estimates. In addition, the 2010 FDA Food Safety Modernization Act includes provisions to increase food safety testing and data collection efforts across the country.

Thousands of Americans suffer from food-borne illnesses every year.

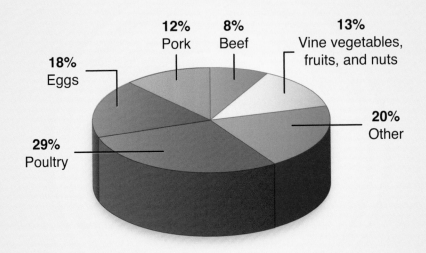

Foods Associated with Salmonella Outbreaks

18% Eggs

12% Pork

8% Beef

13% Vine vegetables, fruits, and nuts

29% Poultry

20% Other

Taken from: www.cdc.gov/VitalSigns/FoodSafety/.

victims require hospitalization. Public health experts also blame salmonella poisoning for about four hundred deaths every year. Nonetheless, the food industry has managed to keep the U.S. government from classifying salmonella as an adulterant—a classification that would force food producers to spend more money on testing and other safety measures.

Salmonella bacteria live in the intestinal tracts of humans and many other animals, including birds, livestock, and pets. Most cases of salmonella poisoning occur when people eat food that is contaminated with animal feces. This contamination usually occurs during food processing, but it can also take place if an infected person handles food with unwashed hands. Contamination can even occur when juices from raw salmonella-tainted meat or poultry make contact with salads, vegetables, fruits, and other ready-to-eat foods.

Victims of food-borne salmonellosis (as salmonella poisoning is sometimes called by doctors) usually experience some combination of fever, diarrhea, and stomach cramps within seventy-two hours of eating the contaminated food. Some people also experience chills, headache, nausea, and vomiting. People usually recover from bouts of salmonella poisoning within four to seven days. For some people, however, salmonella poisoning is more than an unpleasant bout with flu-like symptoms. It is a potential death sentence for people with immune systems that are weakened or not fully developed. Infants and young children, pregnant women and their unborn babies, elderly adults, and people with cancer, diabetes, HIV/AIDS, and other medical conditions are all at heightened risk of dying from salmonella poisoning.

America's Leading Cause of Food-Borne Disease Outbreaks

Although disease outbreaks from salmonella and *E. coli* bacteria are all too common, they actually do not cause as much illness as norovirus. This family of related viruses is the leading cause of food-borne disease outbreaks in the United States. The CDC estimated in 2011 that about 5.5 million Americans are afflicted with a norovirus every year. The CDC estimates that norovirus accounts for about 58 percent of all food-borne illness in the United States, more than all other food-borne bacteria, viruses, and parasites combined.

Fortunately for victims, norovirus is not quite as ferocious as some other food-borne pathogens. People generally recover from norovirus infections within a day or two of medical treatment. Still, the CDC reports that fourteen thousand to fifteen thousand norovirus victims require hospitalization every year—and that 150 Americans die from norovirus annually. As with other food-borne pathogens, norovirus frequently takes a heavier toll on young children, senior citizens, and people who are already in poor health.

People can contract norovirus from contaminated food or drink, touching objects that are contaminated with the virus, or direct contact with an already infected person (such as by sharing a drink or shaking hands). Symptoms of norovirus include nausea, vomiting, and diarrhea, and in some cases infection can erupt into full-blown gastroenteritis (inflammation of the stomach and intestines).

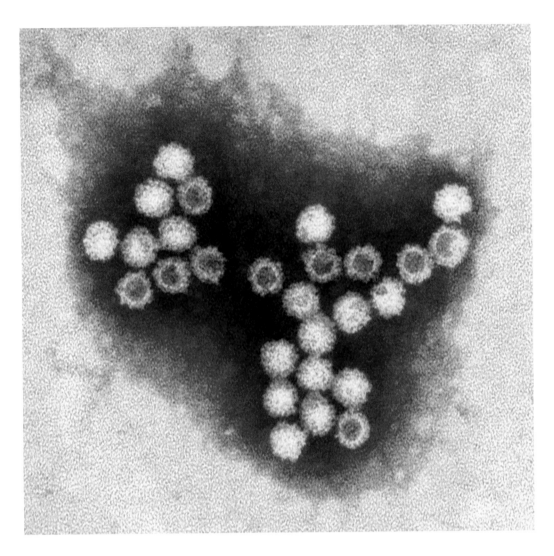

The Fearsome Listeria Bug

A color-enhanced image from an electron micrograph shows particles of norovirus, which is the leading cause of food-borne illnesses in the United States.

Listeria is another food-borne pathogen that has become a dangerous presence in the American food supply. Listeria, for example, was the culprit in a 2011 outbreak of tainted cantaloupe that claimed the lives of twenty-five people in a dozen states. This outbreak ranks as the second-deadliest epidemic of food poisoning in U.S. history. The CDC estimates that listeria accounts for about 250 deaths every year in the United States, even though only about sixteen hundred cases are reported annually. This means that nearly one out of every six people who are afflicted with listeria die from it.

Listeria bacteria are deadly because they are both hardy and hard-hitting. Unlike most bacteria, listeria can grow and multiply in some foods under refrigerated conditions. In addition, listeria germs have the capacity to contaminate a wide variety of raw foods (uncooked meats and produce) and cooked and processed foods (such as soft cheeses, hot dogs, and packaged deli meats). Listeria bacteria are particularly likely to lurk in unpasteurized milk and foods made from unpasteurized milk.

Common symptoms of listeria infection include fever, muscle aches, and diarrhea. Other symptoms sometimes include headache, stiff neck, feelings of confusion, and problems with balance. Physicians and public health experts note, however, that the symptoms of listeria infection can vary significantly from person to person.

Cantaloupes tied to a deadly listeria outbreak in 2001 are left to rot in the fields of a Colorado farm.

Listeria is particularly dangerous for pregnant women. Although many expectant mothers experience little more than a touch of flu-like symptoms from the pathogen, listeria infections often spell serious trouble for the fetuses they carry. Infections during pregnancy can lead to miscarriage, stillbirth, premature delivery, or life-threatening infection of the newborn. Pregnant women are also far more likely to contract a listeria infection than the general population. The CDC estimates, in fact, that pregnant women are twenty times more likely to contract listeriosis (the technical name for a listeria infection) than other healthy adults. Other people at increased risk of death from listeria include newborns and young children, elderly adults, and people with weakened immune systems.

Campylobacter—America's Summertime Menace

Another bacterium that is responsible for a great many cases of food-borne illness is campylobacter. Cases of campylobacteriosis typically soar during the summer months, when warm conditions provide ideal breeding grounds for the bacteria. In addition, most cases of campylobacter infection originate with raw or undercooked chicken, which is a popular summertime food for grilling. Chicken is a key vector for the spread of campylobacter at all times of year, though. The bacteria are easily transmitted through the animal populations of chicken production facilities, and experts assert that food producers have done a poor job of protecting chicken products from this type of contamination. According to the CDC, more than half of the raw chicken sold in the United States is tainted with campylobacter.

Unlike many other food-borne pathogens, campylobacter usually does not cause full-blown outbreaks that sicken dozens or hundreds of people at a time. In most cases the bacteria claim single individuals rather than groups, although campylobacter outbreaks linked to contaminated water and unpasteurized milk have been known to occur. Public health experts say that the rarity of campylobacter outbreaks is due in part to the fact that the germ rarely transfers directly from

A Scary Encounter with *E. coli*

Food-borne illness can strike any time and anywhere, as a fourteen-year-old girl in Utah learned in July 2007. Larissa was midway through an enjoyable stay at summer camp when she suddenly came down with a horrible stomachache and diarrhea that quickly turned bloody. Camp counselors whisked her back home, and her mother rushed her to the local hospital. Tests revealed that Larissa was under attack from *E. coli 0157.H7,* a nasty bacterium that lives in the digestive tract of cows.

Larissa's condition continued to worsen, and before long she was suffering from hemolytic uremic syndrome (HUS), a serious malady that threatens the kidneys. According to doctors, HUS rears its ugly head in up to 10 percent of *E. coli 0157.H7* food poisoning events. The teenager spent the next two weeks in the hospital before she recovered. Meanwhile, authorities combed the summer camp in search of the source of Larissa's illness without success. "We never did find out what it was that I ate [that made me sick]," said Larissa.

Susan Hayes. "Food Fright: Are Food-Safety Systems Doing Enough to Keep Us Safe?" *Current Health 2,* December 2008, p. 18.

one person to another. It is almost always contracted directly from consumption of tainted food or drink. Public health experts have warned, however, that people with undeveloped or weakened immune systems are at special risk of infection.

Most people who contract campylobacter begin to show symptoms within two to five days of exposure. Common symptoms include diarrhea (sometimes bloody), fever, and stomach cramps. Nausea and vomiting also occur in some cases. Campylobacter poisoning usually runs its course in about five to ten days. In rare cases, though, a campylobacter infection also can bring on a terrifying disease called Guillain-Barré syndrome. This rare disorder causes the victim's immune system to start attacking his or her own

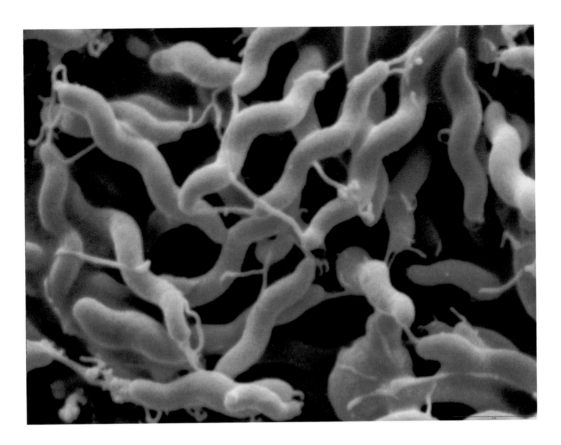

A color-enhanced image from an electron micrograph shows campylobacter bacteria, which are usually associated with the consumption of raw or undercooked chicken.

nervous system. In the worst cases, victims can become virtually paralyzed by the disease to the point that they require medical assistance just to breathe. Most people eventually recover, but the timeline for recovery can range from a few weeks to several years.

In 2011 the CDC reported that the U.S. population experiences about 850,000 cases of food poisoning from campylobacter annually. The bacteria thus accounts for approximately 9 percent of all food-borne illness in the United States. Campylobacteriosis, though, account for about 15 percent of all hospitalizations due to food-borne illness (about eighty-five hundred a year), as well as about 6 percent of all fatalities from food-borne pathogens (about seventy-five a year).

A Never-Ending Battle

Everyone involved in food safety regulation in America recognizes that food-borne bacteria and viruses are always present. Scientists point out, in fact, that bacteria, viruses, fungi, yeasts, and other microorganisms (also known as microbes) have always been—and will always remain—an integral part of life on the planet. "Microbes are everywhere," said food safety expert Marion Nestle. "Around us, on us, and in us. They inhabit soil and water, skin and digestive tract, and any place that provides favorable conditions for growth. . . . Most are harmless, some are even 'friendly,' helping to make bread, wine, vinegar, soy sauce, yogurt, and cheese, and keeping our digestive tracts healthy. Others are less helpful; left to their own devices, they rot apples, mold bread, and spoil meat."[20]

The challenge facing Americans and other people around the world is to take a firmer stand against what Nestle describes as the "unfriendly"[21] microbes: bacteria and viruses that infiltrate food supplies and make people sick. The first key in defending against these pathogens is to appreciate just how formidable they are. Food safety experts, public health officials, and agribusiness researchers all emphasize that the pathogens that dominate the headlines on cable TV news programs and Internet sites are naturally occurring bacteria that have a knack for taking advantage of any opportunity to spread and grow. "Food-borne pathogens are remarkably well-equipped," writes Paul Roberts.

> They are highly potent (a single droplet of blood from a raw chicken contaminated by campylobacter is sufficient to induce fever, cramping, and abdominal pain) and resilient (salmonella can endure freezers). . . . And while most are eventually killed by high temperatures, in some environments, such as raw milk, the normal bacterial load can be so high (with everything from *E. coli* to staphylococcus) that the heat needed for complete sterilization would destroy the food itself. Above all, food-borne pathogens, like all microbes, are quintessential adapters: they can modify their genetics, and thus their physical structure and behavior, to defend themselves against antibiotics and to exploit new opportunities.[22]

FOOD FACT

The United States experiences about 1,000 outbreaks of food-borne illness on an annual basis, according to the Centers for Disease Control and Prevention.

The second step in combating food contamination is to create and implement effective food safety regulations and policies. In a perfect world, these regulations would erect barriers preventing dangerous bacteria and viruses from ever taking up residence in our hamburgers and produce and beverages. We do not live in a perfect world, however, and the food industry complains that some of the solutions to food-borne illness proposed by food safety crusaders would ruin businesses and send grocery bills soaring. Meanwhile, American policymakers also are struggling to keep up with technological developments that are changing the way we raise our food—and in some cases altering the genetic building blocks of food itself.

CHAPTER 4

Fixing the Problem of Food-Borne Illness

A s recently as the 1970s, the American public did not spend a whole lot of time thinking about whether its food supply was safe. Families simply assumed that the beverages and vegetables and meat products spread across their dining room tables were fine. Even if they suffered a bout of food poisoning from some pathogen lurking in the kitchen or the local restaurant, they rarely bothered to notify authorities about their unpleasant experience. Food safety expert Marion Nestle recalled this phenomenon after a disastrous family dinner outing in the 1970s. "Within hours, all but one of us became violently ill," wrote Nestle.

> A flurry of telephone calls the next day made it clear that we were not the only ones who suffered after that dinner. In retrospect, what seems most remarkable about that event was how *ordinary* it was. We survived. We felt better in a day or two. We did not report our illness to health authorities, and neither did anyone else.[23]

Since the 1970s, however, public perceptions about food poisoning have changed enormously. Americans have become less likely to treat food-borne illness as some exotic threat that poses no conceivable harm to them. This shift in attitude is due in large part to an unmistakable rise in the frequency and severity of outbreaks from food-borne pathogens such as salmonella, listeria, and *E. coli* since the 1970s. As these incidents multiplied, local, state, and federal public health agencies took steps to increase their oversight of the food industry.

Despite these efforts, though, illness from food-borne pathogens remains a serious health issue in the United States. In 2011 the Centers for Disease Control and Prevention reported that roughly 48 million Americans—about one out of six people—get sick every year from food-borne diseases. The agency also reported that contaminated food and drink result in 128,000 hospitalizations and three thousand deaths every year. Other studies, meanwhile, indicate that food-related sickness costs Americans billions of dollars annually in health care expenses, lost wages, and higher insurance costs.

Do We Have a Food Safety Crisis?

The results of these studies have spurred intense debate about the state of food safety in the United States. Some scientists, researchers, and consumer advocates believe that the nation is facing a full-blown crisis in food safety, and that consumers should demand major improvements in industry practices. Activist Diane Carmen, for example, expressed disbelief after a 2002 recall of 19 million pounds of hamburger infected with *E. coli* failed to spur any major new food safety regulations. "If 19 million pounds of meat distributed to half of this country had been contaminated with a deadly strain of *E. coli* bacteria by terrorists, we'd go nuts," she wrote. "But when it's done by a Fortune 100 corporation [ConAgra Foods], we continue to buy it and feed it to our kids."[24]

Other observers, though, question whether a crisis even exists. Not surprisingly, the food industry says that the threat of food-borne illness has been exaggerated. This perspective has been echoed by scholars like Terry Etherton, a professor of animal nutrition and animal science at Penn State University. "The story of how agricultural research and contemporary food production practices allow the U.S.

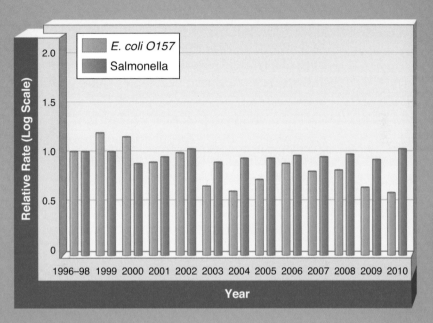

Change in *E. coli O157* and Salmonella Infection Rates, 1996–2010

E. coli O157
Salmonella

Relative Rate (Log Scale)

2.0
1.5
1.0
0.5
0

1996–98 1999 2000 2001 2002 2003 2004 2005 2006 2007 2008 2009 2010

Year

Taken from: www.cdc.gov/VitalSigns/FoodSafety/.

to produce the world's safest food supply is one that tends to get 'lost' in the media frenzy that explodes after a disease outbreak is linked to food," wrote Etherton. "When one looks at the record of foodborne diseases throughout history, it is evident that we have an armada of scientific and public health resources today that are remarkably effective at reducing the risk of contracting disease from food."[25]

Despite such sentiments, however, public skepticism about the safety of our food supply appears to be on the rise. Such doubts have generated renewed demands for additional food safety procedures and regulations. Government officials, consumer advocates, and members of the food industry have all responded to these calls for reform by churning out new ideas to better ensure U.S. food security. As it turns out, however, these groups propose very different solutions.

The Benefits of Proper Cooking and Handling

The big corporations that dominate America's food industry emphasize that food safety can be dramatically improved if consumers follow a few simple rules. Make sure you fully cook meat so that potentially dangerous bacteria are killed. Remember to wash your hands frequently when handling food. Thoroughly wash ready-to-serve fruits (like grapes and strawberries) and vegetables (like carrots and celery) before eating.

These food preparation precautions are sensible and effective in limiting exposure to food-borne pathogens. But it is also in agribusiness's self-interest to push these sorts of consumer-oriented solutions, public health experts and safe-

Ensuring that meat is cooked to a proper temperature will help prevent food-borne illnesses.

food advocates point out. By emphasizing the benefits of proper cooking and handling of food by consumers, corporations at various points along our food pipeline can avoid new safety regulations that diminish their profits. "Maintaining food safety is a cost," wrote food safety advocate Tom Philpott, "and the temptation exists to cut corners."[26]

Critics of agribusiness note, however, that the industry's attempts to place ultimate responsibility for food safety on consumers do not take some important considerations into account. One is that American food consumers have no control over food handling and preparation techniques when they go out to eat, whether at a fast-food joint or a fancy restaurant. Another is that many consumers who do prepare their own food do not fully realize the importance of proper cooking and food handling precautions. As one attorney for victims of food poisoning said, "Consumers assume their food is safe, because otherwise, why would the government let stores sell it?"[27]

Cleaning Up Factory Farms

Much of the criticism of America's food safety focuses on the big meat-production operations that dominate the beef, pork, and poultry industries. These operations, which are known variously as Industrial Animal Feeding Operations (IAFOs), Concentrated Animal Feeding Operations (CAFOs), and "factory farms," house huge numbers of animals in extremely close quarters. These systems enable factory farms to produce large quantities of meat (and dairy products and eggs) very inexpensively. These facilities, though, have also become major breeding grounds for food-borne pathogens like *E. coli,* salmonella, and campylobacter.

The main problem is that livestock crowded into these warehouses pass germs back and forth. According to some estimates, more than half of all feedlot cattle in the United States have *E. coli O157:H7* in their systems. Cows, hogs, chickens, and other livestock also generate large amounts

> # FOOD FACT
>
> In 2002 the U.S. Department of Agriculture approved the use of irradiated meat products in the nation's school lunch programs.

Animals at crowded factory farms such as this hog facility in Missouri are at greater risk of disease, and deadly bacteria tend to develop resistance to antibiotics used to keep the animals healthy.

of waste that is crawling with potentially deadly pathogens. When these tainted feces come into contact with meat during slaughtering and grinding operations, large batches of hamburger and other meats can become contaminated.

Even worse, scientists believe that the dangerous bacteria that thrive in these conditions are becoming harder to kill. The livestock industry makes heavy use of antibiotics to control disease in their tightly packed animal populations. Over time, however, the repeated doses of medicine have had the unintended side-effect of creating new bacterial strains of salmonella, campylobacter, and other food-borne pathogens that are resistant to antibiotics. "With widespread use . . .

antibiotics became less effective because bacteria develop tools to resist them," states one food safety study sponsored by the Center for Science in the Public Interest. "Antibiotics can wipe out most bacteria in a population, but the ones that survive have natural resistance. They reproduce and multiply, and soon the antibiotic has become useless in treating the disease."[28]

Many different proposals for reforming CAFOs—which have also been criticized for being cruel to animals and polluting rivers and lakes—have been made over the years. Consumer advocates, environmentalists, and public health professionals have all urged the passage of new regulations that would limit the size of these facilities, rein in their use of antibiotics, and force them to implement new food safety technologies. All of these proposals have met with staunch opposition from the meat industry.

Better Eating Through Irradiation?

Meatpackers and fast-food companies claim that the best way to reduce sickness from bacteria-tainted meat (besides thorough cooking and frequent hand washing) is through irradiation of meat products. This technology, which has been approved by organizations ranging from the American Medical Association to the World Health Organization, involves treating raw food products with ionizing radiation that kills bacteria and parasites that would otherwise cause food-borne disease. According to the CDC, irradiation technology "holds great potential for preventing many important food-borne diseases that are transmitted through meat, poultry, fresh produce, and other foods. An overwhelming body of scientific evidence demonstrates that irradiation does not harm the nutritional value of food, nor does it make the food unsafe to eat."[29]

Some consumer advocacy and environmental groups strongly oppose irradiation as an industry practice, though. Critics say that irradiated meats and other foods lose some of their nutritional value and do not taste as good. They also worry that if meatpacking companies become dependent on irradiation technology to kill off dangerous pathogens, they will lose all incentive to maintain clean operations and keep animal waste and other contaminants out of the food supply. "I don't want to be served irradiated feces along with my meat," said one veteran food industry journalist.[30]

The USDA requires meat products in the United States that have undergone irradiation to be clearly identified with a radiation label if sold in stores (food services and restaurants are not obligated to provide this information about the food they serve). Since many American consumers see "radiation" as a vaguely scary word, this labeling requirement has severely limited the use of irradiation in the meat industry.

Fully aware of this problem, the food industry began using the phrase "cold pasteurization" rather than "irradiation" to describe the process. Meatpackers have also repeatedly tried to get the USDA to end the labeling requirement. Thus far, however, consumer advocates and other opponents of irradiation have managed to keep the USDA rule in place.

After several days, strawberries that have been irradiated, left, remain fresh compared to a batch that was not similarly treated. Supporters tout irradiation as a way to kill pathogens and improve food safety.

Reducing Industry Influence over Regulators and Policy Makers

Although agribusiness has thus far been unsuccessful in its efforts to weaken or remove irradiation labeling requirements, food safety advocates believe that the industry wields a lot of influence over state and national food policies. They complain that powerful farming, food-processing, grocery, and restaurant groups have made massive campaign contributions to Congress in an effort to derail reforms that might have improved food safety. They point out, for example, that the USDA still does not require the meat industry to test for salmonella, listeria, campylobacter, or other food-borne pathogens besides *E. coli* in their products, despite repeated calls from scientists and food safety advocates. "The main thrust of the industry is profits," explains one retired USDA veterinarian. "You can't add to profits by taking the time to run tests on a product."[31]

The heavy presence of former food industry executives in important government positions also has drawn criticism. "Food companies and trade groups . . . have achieved a remarkable degree of influence in the ways that governors and presidents appoint the regulatory officials who oversee the food industry," writes Paul Roberts. "Top-echelon officials at agencies like the USDA and the FDA often come straight from the ranks of the same food industries those agencies are supposed to regulate."[32]

Concerns about excessive industry influence over food safety policies seem unlikely to decline any time soon. In September 2010 the Union of Concerned Scientists and Iowa State University released the results of a survey of seventeen hundred employees in the Food and Drug Administration and the U.S. Department of Agriculture. More than 620 respondents to the survey—38 percent of the total—agreed or strongly agreed that "public health has been harmed by agency practices that defer to business interests." More than 300 respondents (25 percent) stated that they personally knew of cases in the previous year where the food industry forced their agency to withdraw or significantly modify a policy or action designed to protect consumers from contaminated food. Most respondents to the survey decided to remain anonymous to protect their careers, but one USDA veterinarian agreed to speak out on the record. "Upper-level management does not adequately support field inspectors and the actions they take to protect the food supply," said Dean Wyatt, who manages the agency's slaughterhouse inspectors. "Not only is there lack of support, but there's outright obstruction, retaliation, and abuse of power."[33]

Improving Food Safety One Step at a Time

Advocates for food safety reform admit that the food industry's strong political influence and mammoth size complicate efforts to reduce food-borne illness. They emphasize, however, that even narrowly focused changes to America's vast food delivery system have the capacity to dramatically improve food safety.

For example, regulators and consumer advocates have long argued that outbreaks of food-borne illness could be greatly reduced—both in terms of their number and their severity—if we kept better track of where all our food came from. "The fact that one cow's trimmings can impact hundreds of thousands—or even millions—of pounds of meat is a wake-up call," writes journalist Ezra Klein.

> So too was the [2009] disaster at the Peanut Corporation of America, where some peanuts contaminated with Salmonella typhimurium forced a recall of 3,913 products from 361 companies. That's even scarier than meat: At least you can tell people not to eat a burger, and the advice is fairly easy to follow. It's harder to avoid all processed foods containing compounds laced with peanuts. This is the modern face of tainted food: not a moldy peanut or a piece of rotted meat, but contamination at a production plant that serves hundreds of companies making thousands of foods.[34]

Food safety advocates also say that the United States needs to do a better job of inspecting foods imported from other countries. Imported food makes up an ever-growing

A Tragic Loss Brings New Purpose to a Mother's Life

The ranks of America's crusaders for food safety are dotted with people like Nancy Donley. In 1993 Nancy's six-year-old son Thomas ate a hamburger at a family cookout that was contaminated with *E. coli O157:H7*. Despite the best efforts of medical personnel, Thomas fell terribly ill from the bacteria. As the infection worsened, his kidneys stopped functioning, his brain began swelling, and he suffered a collapsed lung. Four days after eating the contaminated hamburger, the young boy fell into a coma and died in a Chicago hospital.

The death of her only child devastated Nancy, but it also awakened her to the threat of food-borne pathogens in America's food supply. She subsequently joined with other parents whose children had become sick or died from contaminated food to form Safe Tables Our Priority (STOP), an organization dedicated to establishing stronger food safety laws in the United States. "My involvement is in dedication to Alex, who wanted to be a paramedic when he grew up so that 'I can help others,'" Nancy explained. "My desire is to live out my life as Alex would have wanted to live out his own, if it hadn't been cut tragically short."

Quoted in Warren Leon and Caroline Smith DeWaal, with the Center for Science in the Public Interest. *Is Our Food Safe? A Consumer's Guide to Protecting Your Health and the Environment*. New York: Three Rivers Press, 2002, p. 24.

Nancy Donley protests in front of USDA headquarters in 2010.

percentage of the U.S. food supply, yet by some estimates the FDA examines less than 2 percent of the food shipments that come from overseas. This inattention poses a potentially lethal problem for American consumers, especially since food safety regulations in places like China are extremely loose.

Workers at a market in Beijing, China, clear shelves of dairy products after milk tainted with melamine, a toxic chemical, was discovered in that country's food supply, prompting advocates in the United States to question the safety of food from countries without stringent regulations.

In 2007, for example, it was revealed that some Chinese food products were contaminated with a toxic chemical called melamine. "Melamine-tainted milk products sickened hundreds of thousands of infants in China, and melamine contamination is believed to be responsible for thousands of pet deaths in the United States," stated the advocacy group Food and Water Watch. "Melamine adulteration garnered the most headlines, but systemic food safety failures in China have allowed unsafe foods onto global grocery store shelves. The Wild West business environment in China encourages food manufacturers to cut costs and corners. Even Chinese officials have publicly acknowledged their inability to regulate the country's sprawling food production sector."[35]

FOOD FACT

In August 1997 the meat processing company Hudson Foods announced a recall of 35 million pounds of ground beef that had become tainted with *E. coli* at one of its facilities—enough meat, according to food safety expert Eric Schlosser, to provide every single American with a tainted fast-food hamburger.

A Sweeping New Food Safety Law

Consumer advocates and officials in the FDA and USDA say that America's food safety system could be greatly strengthened if federal and state food safety agencies simply received additional funding to hire more researchers and inspectors. They point out that the number of food inspectors in the USDA and FDA fell steadily during the 1980s and 1990s, which meant a decline in food safety inspections as well. The number of USDA employees responsible for monitoring food safety in the meat and poultry industries, for example, fell from twelve thousand in 1978 to seventy-five hundred in 1997. This level of staffing has remained fairly constant ever since, even as mass food poisonings from salmonella, listeria, and *E. coli* continue to garner news headlines.

In 2010 the U.S. Congress increased food safety inspection by passing the FDA Food Safety Modernization Act, the most sweeping food safety legislation in more than seventy years. This legislation, which was signed into law by President Barack Obama in January 2011, paved the way for hiring as many as two thousand new FDA inspectors. Many consumer advocates, food experts, and FDA employees, though, believe that the act's other features will have an even greater impact on food safety. For the first time ever, the law gives the FDA the power to order recalls of contaminated foods. Before, food companies could decide for themselves whether to issue product recalls. It also requires farming operations and food-processing facilities to implement new food safety plans, and it gives the FDA access to internal records at farms and food-production facilities. The law also requires importers to verify that food products grown or processed overseas meet all U.S. safety standards.

Even supporters of the FDA Food Safety Modernization Act admit that the law is not perfect. For one thing, it does

President Obama signs the FDA Food Safety Modernization Act in 2011. The law is considered the most sweeping food safety legislation enacted in seventy years.

Debating the Merits of a Single Food Safety Agency

Under the current U.S. system, government responsibilities for food safety are divided among multiple agencies. Many critics claim that this system is confusing and inefficient. "A sandwich made with bread, ham, cheese, lettuce, and tomato raises regulatory issues of terrifying complexity," wrote food safety scholar Marion Nestle. "If the sandwich is made with one slice of bread, it falls under USDA rules [because it is considered a meat or poultry item]; if it is made with two slices, it is the FDA's responsibility [because the meat is not visible]. To protect the safety of such a sandwich, three cabinet-level federal agencies—the FDA, EPA, and USDA (including four major divisions of the latter)—oversee its farm-to-table production."

Some food safety advocates have argued that the U.S. government could more effectively manage its food safety obligations if it moved all of the food-related work of the USDA, FDA, EPA, and other departments into a single federal agency. Supporters of a single federal Department of Food say that establishing such an agency would make it much easier for the food industry to understand and obey food safety regulations. Even more importantly, such an agency might dramatically improve the safety of the foods and drinks that Americans consume every day. "A single agency would be able to develop transparent safety standards, consolidate and prioritize food safety programs, and coordinate the federal response to outbreaks of food contamination," said one policy analyst at the Center for Food Safety, a public health advocacy group.

Marion Nestle. *Safe Food: Bacteria, Biotechnology, and Bioterrorism.* Berkeley: University of California Press, 2003, p. 57.

New York Times Editors. "Do We Need a Department of Food?" *Room for Debate* (blog), February 8, 2009. http:// roomfordebate.blogs.nytimes.com/2009/02/08/do-we -need-a-department-of-food/.

not include food safety provisions for the meat and poultry industries, which remain under the supervision of the USDA. Public health experts believe, though, that the law represents a welcome change in America's food safety priorities. "This bill requires a fundamental shift in the FDA's food safety program from reacting to illnesses and deaths to preventing them in the first place," said Chris Waldrop, director of the Food Policy Institute at the Consumer Federation of America.[36]

CHAPTER 5

Food Safety in the Twenty-First Century

When it comes to food supply issues, food-borne infections grab the most headlines in the United States and other developed countries around the world. Public health experts, physicians, and consumer advocates, however, have also expressed safety concerns about other aspects of food production. As advances in science and technology sweep through the food industry, these concerns have intensified.

Pesticide Residues on Food

Food growers in the United States and other countries make extensive use of pesticides to protect their crops from harmful insects and damaging weeds during the growing and harvest seasons, as well as during the storage and transportation phases. Pesticides allow farmers to increase the amount of usable food they can raise, and these chemicals can improve the quality, safety, and shelf-life of certain foods.

The Environmental Protection Agency (EPA) has imposed limits on the amount and types of pesticides that growers can use on their crops. Restrictions have been put in place for chemicals that kill crop-destroying bugs (known as insecticides), weeds and other vegetation threats (herbicides), and damaging fungi (fungicides). These restrictions are designed to keep growers from using pesticides to the point that they actually make the food unhealthy or dangerous to eat. Nonetheless, some observers believe that current limitations—also known as tolerances—for pesticide residues on crops and feed are too weak.

A tractor moves through a Florida strawberry field spraying fungicide and pesticide. Critics maintain that EPA regulations on the amount and type of pesticides that farmers can use are inadequate.

Most critics who say that there is too much pesticide residue in the food supply admit that individual strawberries, carrots, grapes, apples, peaches, corn, and other crops contain very little insecticide residue. The problem, say some public health and environmental groups, is that regulatory agencies have not sufficiently researched the *cumulative* health impact of ingesting insecticide residues. Food safety organizations like the Pesticide Action Network also point out that "U.S. EPA sets limits on the maximum amount of each pesticide that can be on each food item, . . . [but] there's no limit to the number of different pesticides that can be on your food, or the total amount of contamination."[37]

Families worried about pesticides in their food have several options to reduce their exposure. Food safety advocates say that thoroughly washing and peeling fruits and vegetables (using a drop or two of dish soap and cold water for rinsing) can get rid of a lot of pesticide residue. In addition, food safety experts like Warren Leon and Caroline Smith DeWaal note that "choosing foods with little or no pesticide residues is getting easier and easier as organic products boasting a new national [USDA organic] label arrive at your local market. . . . Many parents can significantly reduce their children's pesticide exposure by switching to organically grown apples, peaches, and strawberries."[38]

FOOD FACT

Public opinion polls indicate that nine out of ten Americans would like all genetically modified foods to be labeled, but as of 2011 the FDA had made no such requirement.

If your family is unable or unwilling to buy organic produce, however, medical professionals and food safety advocates agree that adults and children alike should still eat plenty of fruits and vegetables. The Environmental Working Group (EWG) is an organization that is devoted to reducing pesticide levels in our food supply. The EWG, though, firmly states that "the health benefits of a diet rich in fruits and vegetables outweigh the risks of pesticide exposure. . . . Eating conventionally-grown produce is far better than not eating fruits and vegetables at all."[39]

Early Puberty and America's Food Supply

During the 1980s and 1990s doctors, parents, scientists, and food safety advocates became tangled in a heated debate that remains with us today. The debate centers on whether high rates of consumption of milk and certain other foods are partly responsible for the rise in "precocious puberty"—a phenomenon in which girls and boys enter puberty at an unusually early age.

There is widespread agreement about some of the factors that are contributing to this trend, which is also sometimes called early-onset puberty. Rising rates of obesity, declining rates of exercise, and exposure to industrial chemicals (such as those used in plastics manufacturing) are all responsible to some degree for the rising percentage of girls and boys who are entering puberty at an early age—six or seven in some cases.

Some observers question whether early-onset puberty among girls and boys can be tied to traces of artificial hormones in the milk they drink.

The Dirty Dozen and the Clean Fifteen

In 2011 the Environmental Working Group (EWG) released a study of pesticide contamination of 53 popular fruits and vegetables sold in the United States. The EWG analyzed the results of fifty-one thousand tests for pesticides on these foods conducted from 2000 to 2009 by the U.S. Department of Agriculture and the Food and Drug Administration. The EWG then publicized a "dirty dozen" list of fruits and vegetables found to be most contaminated by pesticides, as well as a "clean fifteen" list of produce found to have the smallest traces of pesticides.

Dirty Dozen

1. Apples
2. Celery
3. Strawberries
4. Peaches
5. Spinach
6. Nectarines (imported)
7. Grapes (imported)
8. Sweet bell peppers
9. Potatoes
10. Blueberries
11. Lettuce
12. Kale/collard greens

Clean Fifteen

1. Onions
2. Sweet corn
3. Pineapples
4. Avocado
5. Asparagus
6. Sweet Peas
7. Mangoes
8. Eggplant
9. Cantaloupe
10. Kiwi
11. Cabbage
12. Watermelon
13. Sweet potatoes
14. Grapefruit
15. Mushrooms

Environmental Working Group. *EWG 2011 Shopper's Guide to Pesticides in Produce.* www.ewg.org/foodnews/summary/.

Apples have been found to contain the highest levels of pesticides compared with other produce items.

Some people believe that earlier puberty can also be linked to the mid-1990s, when the dairy industry began using artificial growth hormones in their cows. According to this theory, traces of those growth hormones are being passed along to young girls and boys through milk and other dairy products (consumption of hormone-treated meat products have also been blamed for early puberty). This theory has been widely discussed in all sorts of media, from environmental and public health magazines to parenting websites. In some cases, the milk–early puberty link has even been described as a scientifically proven one. In 2007, for example, Diane Marty wrote in *E: The Environmental Magazine* that "more and more evidence points to a relationship between hormones in milk and early puberty in teens, preteens and even grade schoolers. If you buy only one organic item for your kids, make it milk."[40]

In reality, though, many researchers doubt any link exists between the consumption of hormone-laced dairy products and precocious puberty. "This is how myths start," said Ruth Kava, director of nutrition for the American Council on Science and Health. "There have always been hormones in milk, and American girls have always had milk in their diets, so why would that cause a change in puberty all of a sudden?"[41]

Scientists say that milk-boosting hormones given to cows are mostly destroyed when their milk is pasteurized. Researchers also note that nations that forbid the use of growth hormones in their dairy herds, such as Canada and countries in the European Union, are seeing the same rise in early-onset puberty that the United States is experiencing. Finally, tests conducted by the Food and Drug Administration have concluded that there is no difference between milk produced by cows treated with growth hormones and those not treated with growth hormones.

Better Food Through Bioengineering?

The debates over the presence of pesticides and artificial growth hormones in our food supply are unlikely to end anytime soon. To some degree, however, both of these controversies have been overshadowed by yet another debate

Signs mark the locations of different varieties of genetically modified corn growing in Wisconsin. As of 2011, around 90 percent of the corn, soybeans, and cotton grown in the United States came from GM seeds.

about the role of modern technology and science in the raising of food. The issue in question concerns the manipulation of genes—the building blocks of all life—to create new varieties of crops that grow more quickly, yield more food, and stay fresh longer. This high-tech food-growing method is variously known as genetic modification, bioengineering, and transgenic technology. However it is labeled, though, the practice has divided consumers, scientists, environmental and public health organizations, and dietary experts into warring camps.

Genetically modified (GM) foods have been sold commercially in the United States since 1993, when the Food and Drug Administration determined that GM products should be treated no differently than those produced by traditional farming methods. "The key factors in reviewing safety concerns [about food]," said the FDA, "should be

the characteristics of the food product, rather than the fact that new methods are used."[42] Many environmental groups, consumer advocates, and scientists harshly condemned this ruling. They charged that no one—including the FDA—really knew whether bioengineered food was healthy and safe over the passage of years.

By the mid-1990s farmers all across the country were raising fields full of bioengineered corn, soybeans, cotton, and other crops. GM foods have increased in popularity ever since. By 2011 around 90 percent of America's corn, soybeans, and cotton were produced from GM seeds. Many other U.S. fruits and vegetables are now commonly produced through bioengineering as well. In 2011 federal authorities estimated that 60 to 70 percent of all processed foods on supermarket shelves contain genetically engineered ingredients.

American farmers are not the only ones using GM seeds, either. Some nations, such as Canada, Japan, and the countries of the European Union (EU), have passed strict laws against bioengineered foods. Others, however, have embraced the technology. By the late 2000s, in fact, GM crops were being cultivated in 22 countries by over 10 million farmers. About 9 million of these farmers, wrote British politician and GM foods supporter Dick Taverne, "are resource-poor farmers in developing countries, mainly India and China. Most of these small-scale farmers grow pest-resistant GM cotton. . . . This cotton benefits farmers because it reduces the need for insecticides, thereby increasing their income and also improving their health."[43]

Touting the Benefits of GM Foods

Supporters say that transgenic foods have benefits that can make the world a healthier and better place. Advocates frequently claim that the technology could prove essential in feeding a planet that grows more heavily populated with each passing day. After all, GM seeds produce much larger

> # FOOD FACT
>
> The blood of the average American contains traces of 212 different industrial chemicals, according to the Centers for Disease Control and Prevention.

volumes of food than non-GM seeds. This means that farmers can generate much more food without expanding the size of their fields. In addition, researchers are working on genetically engineered crops capable of thriving in dry or cold environments. Such crops would be a great help to nations that have a limited supply of good farmland.

Another promising avenue of research lies in the development of foods that are genetically designed to carry extra health benefits. GM supporters say that this technology has the capacity to pack extra vitamins and nutrients into bananas, rice, spinach, and other foods. Such products could improve the health and vitality not only of American children and adults, but of poor people around the world who have limited access to nutritious food. Champions of GM foods also claim that genetic engineering could eventually produce fruits and vegetables that inoculate consumers against a wide range of diseases and health problems.

Finally, advocates of food bioengineering claim that the technology has many environmental benefits. For example, some pest-resistant GM crops do not require as much spraying with herbicides or insecticides, which can pollute rivers, lakes, and groundwater resources. In addition, the high yields associated with GM crops have the potential to benefit natural ecosystems that support wildlife by reducing the amount of land needed for farming.

Criticisms of GM Foods

Most opponents of transgenic technology acknowledge that GM foods have some attractive features. They feel, however, that the potential drawbacks far outweigh the benefits. They also insist that it is much too early to predict what all of those drawbacks may be. As food safety expert Marion Nestle writes, "Transgenic foods raise safety issues that are difficult to define, predict, or quantify [measure] but that nevertheless should be taken seriously and evaluated in advance—*before* the foods are grown extensively and enter the food supply."[44]

GM opponents believe that the rise of transgenic crops poses a number of potential threats to the environment. They worry that the genes contained in "mutant" foods will intermingle with and eventually destroy naturally occur-

Protesters voice their objections to GM foods at a demonstration in Chicago, Illinois. Critics are concerned about the health and environmental impact of GM foods.

ring species of fruits and vegetables—as well as the animal species that depend on them. In addition, critics assert that some GM crops have unintended side effects on certain animals. There have been claims, for example, that pollen from transgenic corn has contributed to the decline in America's endangered monarch butterfly population.

Most of the criticisms of GM foods, though, center on human health factors. Many critics believe that new bioengineered strains of food might cause new food allergies. "The government does not require biotechnology companies to test for allergens, and they rarely do," writes Nestle. "For one thing, testing is difficult. For another, testing is hardly in a company's best interest. . . . Like testing for microbial pathogens, testing for allergens is risky: you might find one."[45]

Other complaints about the growing presence of GM products in the food supply focus on potential health problems that have yet to reveal themselves. Critics argue that we do not yet know whether eating transgenic foods might cause health problems twenty, thirty, or forty years down the road. For this reason, anti-GM groups and researchers have continually called on Congress, the FDA, and the USDA to monitor the industry much more closely and insist on greater levels of testing. "There has been a complete abdication [surrender] of any responsible legislative or regulatory oversight of genetically engineered foods," declared the Center for Food Safety, a public health and environmental advocacy organization. "Clearly, now is a critical time to challenge the government's negligence in managing the human health and environmental threats from biotechnology."[46]

A New Age of Genetically Engineered Animals

The battle over GM foods has taken another turn in recent years with the emergence of genetically modified animals. Researchers in China have created genetically altered cows that produce milk with the same nutritional properties as human breast milk. Scientists in Canada have unveiled GM pigs that produce manure that is far less damaging to nearby rivers and streams than that of regular pigs. Meanwhile, some people say that it is only a matter of time before GM animals revolutionize the practice of medicine. "Pigs engineered for human tissue compatibility might someday cut short the agonizingly long wait patients now have for organ transplants," writes journalist Jason Best.

> Drugs that cost six figures per year to synthesize for a single sufferer of a rare disease such as hemophilia might be produced much more cheaply in the bodies of GM mice. There are even potential environmental benefits to some genetically altered animals: tiny fish that produce a light-emitting enzyme and glow when exposed to certain pollutants, plants engineered to suck toxic metals out of contaminated soils.[47]

Public support for using bioengineering for medical research has been consistently strong. When it comes to *eating* GM animals, though, many people are far more queasy. They dislike the idea of eating pork chops or steaks that come from a genetically altered animal—in part because GM opponents have raised doubts about the long-term wisdom of transgenic technology. Bioengineering supporters, though, say that the technology has the potential to increase the supply of safe, inexpensive, and nutritious meat, fish, and poultry in the United States and around the world.

Salmon sits on ice at Pike Place Fish Market in Seattle, Washington. In 2011, the FDA made the controversial recommendation that a company behind the creation of a GM salmon be approved to sell its product in the United States.

A Harrowing Encounter with Pesticide Drift

Many people worry about health threats from food laced with pesticides. People can also become ill, however, from absorbing pesticide residues from orchards and fields through the skin. In eastern Washington, for example, middle-school student Elena Dominguez began suffering a variety of mysterious health ailments, including seizures and fainting spells. Her mother, Cindy, suspected that her daughter's difficulties might have been due to pesticides that were being sprayed on apple orchards next to her school. Cindy contacted the U.S. Department of Agriculture with her concerns, and USDA investigators subsequently found pesticide residues on Elena's gym clothes as well as the school playground and track field. The investigators and Elena's doctors decided that she was a victim of pesticide poisoning.

"I was relieved to finally get an answer," said Cindy, who from that point on made sure that her children stayed indoors when local orchards did their pesticide spraying. "But my neighbors' kids were still out there. . . . There was something inside me that said, 'I have to do something. This is so wrong. Children are playing in [pesticide] drift zones.'" When Cindy first asked the school district to adopt policies to protect school children from drifting pesticide residues, she was ignored. But when she threatened to take legal action, the school district took notice. Administrators secured a promise from the neighboring orchard owners to inform the school whenever they were planning a pesticide treatment so that the school could keep kids inside.

Ariana Kelly. "One Mom's Story About Pesticide Drift Near Schools." Moms Rising.org, February 18, 2010. www.momsrising.org/blog/one-moms-story-about-pesticide-drift-near-schools/.

In the United States, the debate over whether to permit commercial sale of GM animals for the dinner table has centered for several years on the so-called AquAdvantage salmon. This genetically engineered fish grows much more quickly—and to a much greater size—than ordinary Atlantic salmon. The fish was created by scientists at a Massachusetts-based company called AquaBounty Technologies, which has asked the Food and Drug Administration for approval to sell it to stores, restaurants, and food services across the United States.

AquaBounty and supporters of GM foods claim that the genetically engineered AquAdvantage fish is just as tasty, nutritious, and safe to eat as wild salmon. They also assert that the introduction of transgenic salmon and other fish could relieve pressure on wild fish populations, some of which are being harvested to near extinction. In the last half-century, in fact, annual global seafood consumption has jumped from 22 pounds per person to 38 pounds. So-called "fish farms"—companies that raise captive fish in tanks and other enclosures—have helped meet some of this increased demand, but industry observers say that wild fishing populations still bear the brunt of the rising appetite for seafood. "The wild stocks [of fish] are not going to keep up," said Stephen Hall, director general of the WorldFish Center, a fisheries research group. "Something else has to fill that gap."[48]

Opponents of commercial sale of the AquAdvantage salmon say that a far better approach to protecting wild fish populations would be to reduce the amount of fish that the fishing industry is allowed to catch each year. They also warn that if GM salmon were to escape and mate with wild salmon (as farm-raised fish sometimes do), they might forever change the genetic character of the wild fish. These "Frankenfish," according to journalist Timothy Egan, would result in

> fast fish from the factory, without the hassle of habitat preservation. I'm not reflexively afraid of living better through chemistry. Genetically modified corn and soybeans have been around for some time. If we can grow food and fiber with less demand on water and nutrients, that's often worth pursuing. But the Frankenfish is a much bigger step, and not just because it opens the door to federal approval of all kinds of freaks from the farm.[49]

Finally, some critics assert that without further testing, no one really knows whether people who eat GM salmon or other bioengineered foods will suffer unforeseen health problems in years to come.

Despite these concerns, the FDA in 2011 recommended approval of the AquAdvantage salmon for human consumption on the U.S. market. The FDA's decision was a great disappointment to anti-GM activists. They now say that if the government is going to allow GM salmon and other bioengineered meat products on grocery store shelves, they should at least be labeled as transgenic so that consumers can decide for themselves whether to purchase GM or non-GM foods. Not surprisingly, AquaBounty and other companies involved in GM food production oppose such labeling requirements.

Whatever the outcome of the struggle over GM labeling, it is clear that the United States—and much of the rest of the world—has entered a new age of agriculture. As Nestle puts it, "Genetically modified foods *already* pervade the food supply. The experiment is in progress; its results will emerge in due course. Whether such an experiment is in the public interest—or for that matter is in the interest of the industry—will also be revealed in time."[50]

NOTES

Chapter 1: The History of U.S. Food Safety

1. Quoted in Carol Ballentine. "Taste of Raspberries, Taste of Death: The 1937 Elixir Sulfanilamide Incident." *FDA Consumer,* June 1981. www.fda.gov/AboutFDA/WhatWeDo/History/ProductRegulation/SulfanilamideDisaster/default.htm.

2. Quoted in Timothy Egan. *The Worst Hard Time.* Boston: Houghton Mifflin, 2006, p. 256.

3. Michael Pollan. *The Omnivore's Dilemma: A Natural History of Four Meals.* New York: Penguin Books, 2006, p. 49.

4. Charlotte Freeman. "Buying the Farm: Planting the Seeds of Agricultural Bliss." Culinate.com, May 14, 2008. www.culinate.com/articles/first_person/family_farm.

5. Bill Clinton. "Remarks on Signing the Food Quality Protection Act of 1996." August 3, 1996. The American Presidency Project. www.presidency.ucsb.edu/ws/?pid=53155.

6. Quoted in interview with Doug Hamilton. *Frontline, "Modern Meat."* PBS, 2002. www.pbs.org/wgbh/pages/frontline/shows/meat/interviews/tauxe.html.

7. Eric Schlosser. *Fast Food Nation: The Dark Side of the All-American Meal.* New York: Houghton Mifflin, 2001, p. 196.

8. Paul Roberts. *The End of Food.* New York: Houghton Mifflin, 2008, p. 178.

9. Quoted in Roberts, *The End of Food,* p. 181.

10. Nicols Fox. *Spoiled: The Dangerous Truth About a Food Chain Gone Haywire.* New York: Penguin Books, 1997, p. 8.

11. Quoted in Christopher D. Cook. *Diet for a Dead Planet: How the Food Industry Is Killing Us.* New York: New Press, 2004, p. 49.

12. Quoted in Lyndsey Layton. "House Passes Legislation Overhauling Food-Safety Laws." *Washington Post,* December 21, 2010. www.washingtonpost.com/wp-dyn/content/article/2010/12/21/AR2010122104646.html.

Chapter 2: Guardians of Food Safety in America

13. James T. O'Reilly. *A Consumer's Guide to Food Regulation and Safety.* New York: Oceana/Oxford University Press, 2010, pp. 9–10.

14. Renée Johnson. "The Federal Food Safety System: A Primer." *Congressional Research Service (CRS) Report for Congress*. Washington, DC: CRS, January 11, 2011, p. 4.
15. O'Reilly. *A Consumer's Guide to Food Regulation and Safety*, p. 10.

Chapter 3: The Food-Borne Germs That Make Us Sick

16. Quoted in Madeline Dexter. "Why Your Food Isn't Safe." *Good Housekeeping*, September 12, 2011. www.goodhousekeeping.com/health/womens-health/how-to-keep-food-safe.
17. Dexter. "Why Your Food Isn't Safe."
18. Quoted in Pat Curtis. "Iowa Woman Part of Washington Food Safety Rally." RadioIowa.com, October 21, 2011. www.radioiowa.com/2010/03/17/iowa-woman-part-of-washington-food-safety-rally/.
19. Roberts. *The End of Food*, p. 180.
20. Marion Nestle. *Safe Food: Bacteria, Biotechnology, and Bioterrorism*. Berkeley: University of California Press, 2003, p. 35.
21. Nestle. *Safe Food*, p. 35.
22. Roberts. *The End of Food*, pp. 178–179.

Chapter 4: Fixing the Problem of Food-Borne Illness

23. Nestle. *Safe Food*, p. 33.
24. Diane Carmen. "Just Cook the Crud Out of It." *Denver Post*, July 25, 2002. www.purefood.org/Toxic/ecoli0702.cfm.
25. Terry Etherton. "Food Safety: Then and Now." *Feedstuffs*, August 15, 2011, p. 9.
26. Quoted in "Do We Really Have a Food-Safety Crisis?" *Grist*, November 9, 2010. www.grist.org/article/food-2010-11-09-do-we-really-have-a-food-safety-crisis.
27. Quoted in Roberts. *The End of Food*, p. 188.
28. Warren Leon and Caroline Smith DeWaal, with the Center for Science in the Public Interest. *Is Our Food Safe? A Consumer's Guide to Protecting Your Health and the Environment*. New York: Three Rivers Press, 2002, p. 27.
29. Centers for Disease Control and Prevention. "Food Irradiation: FAQs," October 11, 2005. www.cdc.gov/ncidod/dbmd/diseaseinfo/foodirradiation.htm#cdcposition.
30. Quoted in Schlosser. *Fast Food Nation*, p. 218.
31. Quoted in Michael Janofsky. "U.S. Hopeful on Food Safety Efforts, but Critics Are Skeptical." *New York Times*, August 21, 1997. www.nytimes.com/1997/08/21/us/us-hopeful-on-food-safety-efforts-but-critics-are-skeptical.html?pagewanted=all&src=pm.
32. Roberts. *The End of Food*, p. 293.
33. Union of Concerned Scientists "FDA and USDA Scientists Say U.S. Food System Needs Strengthening:

Hundreds Say Corporations Wield Undue Influence." Press release, September 13, 2010. www.ucsusa .org/news/press_release/fda-and -usda-scientists-survey-0402.html.

34. Ezra Klein. "Where's the Beef (Coming From)?" *Washington Post,* October 6, 2009. www.voices.washing tonpost.com/ezra-klein/2009/10 /the_times_titled_this_article.html.

35. Food and Water Watch. "A Decade of Dangerous Food Imports from China," June 8, 2011. www.food andwaterwatch.org/reports/a-de cade-of-dangerous-food-imports -from-china/.

36. Quoted in Helena Bottemiller. "Food Safety Bill Heads to President's Desk." *Food Safety News,* December 22, 2010. www.foodsafe tynews.com/2010/12/food-safety -bill-clear-final-hurdle-heads-for -presidents-desk/.

Chapter 5: Food Safety in the Twenty-First Century

37. Pesticide Action Network. "Your Health: Food." N.d. www.panna .org/your-health/food.

38. Leon and DeWaal. *Is Our Food Safe?* p. 102.

39. Environmental Working Group. *EWG's Shoppers' Guide to Pesticides.* 2011. www.ewg.org/food news/summary/.

40. Diane Marty. "Empowered Shopping: Tips from the Green Side of the Aisle." *E: The Environmental Magazine,* April 30, 2007. www .emagazine.com/archive/3714.

41. Quoted in Lisa Belkin. "The Making of an 8-Year-Old Woman. *New York Times Magazine,* December 24, 2000, p. 38.

42. Food and Drug Administration. "Statement of Policy: Foods Derived from New Plant Varieties"; Notice. Part 9. *Federal Register,* vol. 57, no. 104. Washington, DC: Government Printing Office, May 29, 1992, pp. 22,984–22,985.

43. Dick Taverne. "The Real GM Food Scandal." *Prospect,* November 25, 2007. www.prospectmagazine .co.uk/2007/11/therealgmfood scandal/.

44. Nestle. *Safe Food,* p. 185.

45. Nestle. *Safe Food,* p. 173.

46. Center for Food Safety. "Genetically Engineered Crops." n.d. www .centerforfoodsafety.org/campaign /genetically-engineered-food /crops/.

47. Jason Best. "The Splice Age." *OnEarth,* Winter 2003, p. 24.

48. Quoted in Bryan Walsh, "The End of the Line," *Time,* July 18, 2011, pp. 29–36.

49. Timothy Egan. "Frankenfish Phobia." *New York Times,* March 17, 2011. www.opinionator.blogs. nytimes.com/2011/03/17/franken fish-phobia.

50. Nestle. *Safe Food,* p. 192–03.

adulteration: The addition of impure or inferior ingredients, usually in secrecy.

agribusiness: Any business or industry that is involved in some part of food production.

antibiotics: Medical drugs used to treat bacterial infections.

bacteria: Single-celled microorganisms, some of which can cause disease.

herbicide: A type of pesticide used specifically to kill weeds or other undesirable plants.

microbe: A microorganism that causes disease.

pathogen: Bacteria or virus that causes disease.

perishable: Foods that spoil quickly or easily.

pesticide: Chemical used to kill insects, weeds, and other pests.

processed: Food that has been altered from its original state to make it tastier, easier, or more convenient to eat, such as through the addition of chemical preservatives.

regulation: Rules and laws designed to guide how individuals or businesses conduct themselves.

standard: A required level of safety or quality.

vector: Carrier of disease.

ORGANIZATIONS TO CONTACT

American Meat Institute (AMI)

1150 Connecticut Ave. NW
12th Fl.
Washington, DC 20036
phone: (202) 587-4200
website: www.meatami.com

AMI is the country's oldest and largest meat and poultry trade association. It serves as the leading voice of American meat and poultry producers on all issues that affect its members, including safety and regulation matters. One of the organization's top priorities is to address "myths" about the meat and poultry industries and help consumers "make informed choices" that are right for them.

Center for Food Safety

660 Pennsylvania Ave. SE
Suite 302
Washington, DC 20003
phone: (202) 547-9359
website: www.centerforfoodsafety.org

The Center for Food Safety describes itself as a nonprofit organization devoted to protecting human health and the environment by opposing genetically modified food and other "harmful" food production technologies. The center also champions organic food production and other sustainable forms of agriculture.

Food and Water Watch

1616 P St., NW
Suite 300
Washington, DC 20036
phone: (202) 683-2500
website: www.foodandwaterwatch.org

Food and Water Watch is a nonprofit consumer safety organization that monitors food and water quality throughout the United States and around the world. The group works to shape food and water regulations through a combination of education programs and lobbying efforts.

STOP Foodborne Illness

3759 N. Ravenswood Ave., Suite 224
Chicago, IL 60613
phone: (773) 269-6555
website: www.stopfoodborneillness.org

Formerly known as Safe Tables Our Priority (STOP), STOP Foodborne Illness is dedicated to reducing foodborne illness and death across the United States. The organization's priorities range from stronger regulation of the food industry to helping people struggling with health problems from food poisoning.

U.S. Department of Agriculture (USDA)

1400 Independence Ave. SW
Washington, DC 20250
phone: (202) 720-2791
website: www.usda.gov

The USDA is the federal agency that bears primary responsibility for regulating meat and dairy products in the United States. The USDA also has many other responsibilities, including management of America's school lunch program to stewardship of its national forests. It remains best known, however, for its role as a regulator and supporter of American farms. The USDA website includes all sorts of information on various aspects of U.S. agriculture and food safety.

U.S. Food and Drug Administration (FDA)

10903 New Hampshire Ave.
Silver Spring, MD 20993
phone: (888) 463-6332
website: www.fda.gov

The FDA is the federal agency primarily responsible for ensuring the safety of America's food supply. The agency maintains a website that provides consumers with all sorts of detailed information on food regulation issues ranging from nutrition labeling requirements to information on dietary supplements and genetically modified foods.

FOR MORE INFORMATION

Books and Articles

Grist. "Food Fight: Do We Really Have a Food Safety Crisis?" November 9, 2010. www.grist.org/article/food -2010-11-09-do-we-really-have-a -food-safety-crisis. A group of food industry scholars and consumer advocates engage in a spirited debate about the state of food regulation and safety in the United States.

Marc T. Law. "History of Food and Drug Regulation in the United States." *EH.NET Encyclopedia of Economic and Business History,* October 2004. http://eh.net/encyclopedia/article /Law.Food.and.Drug.Regulation. Provides a clear and informative overview of the ways in which U.S. regulation of the food and drug industries have changed since the colonial era.

Warren Leon and Caroline Smith DeWaal, with the Center for Science in the Public Interest. *Is Our Food Safe? A Consumer's Guide to Protecting Your Health and the Environment.* New York: Three Rivers Press, 2002. Provides a wide-ranging discussion of various food safety issues and offers recommendations for making sure that the food you eat is safe and nutritious.

Michael Moss. "The Burger That Shattered Her Life." *New York Times,* October 3, 2009. www.nytimes.com /2009/10/04/health/04meat.html ?pagewanted=all. Tells the frightening story of Stephanie Smith, a young Minneapolis dance instructor who was left paralyzed after she ate a hamburger contaminated with *E. coli* virus.

Michael Pollan. *The Omnivore's Dilemma for Kids.* New York: Dial, 2009. A kids' version of a best-selling book by one of America's most prominent food industry experts.

Victoria Sherrow. *Food Safety.* New York: Chelsea House, 2008. Arranged in point/counterpoint fashion, this book discusses whether agricultural pesticides and genetically modified foods pose threats to human health or the environment.

Websites

Fight BAC! Keep Food Safe from Bacteria (www.fightbac.org). This website is maintained by the Partnership for Food Safety Education, which includes both consumer safety groups and food industry associations. It includes tips on handling food safely, educating kids about how food-borne illnesses are transmitted, and other consumer-targeted information.

Food Allergy and Anaphylaxis Network (www.foodallergy.org). Provides a wide range of resources related to food allergies, including education, research, and advocacy programs.

Food Safety at CDC (www.cdc.gov /foodsafety). Provides detailed information on outbreaks of foodborne illness, as well as details on government food safety programs and regulations.

FoodSafety.gov. This website serves as a gateway to food safety information and alerts from all of the nation's leading food safety agencies, including the Food Safety and Inspection Service (FSIS) of the U.S. Department of Agriculture, the U.S. Food and Drug Administration (FDA), and the Centers for Disease Control and Prevention (CDC).

Food Safety Project (www.extension .iastate.edu/foodsafety). This comprehensive website maintained by Iowa State University is dedicated to "food safety from farm to table." It includes information on safe food handling, trends in food-borne illness, and breaking food safety stories.

Home Food Safety (www.homefood safety.org). A joint effort of the American Dietetic Assocation and the ConAgra food company, this website provides home food safety statistics, information about various types of food-borne illness, and safe food handling information and tips.

NSF Scrub Club (www.scrubclub .org). The National Science Foundation operates this website dedicated to educating kids about the importance of hand washing in stopping food-borne illness. The site includes multimedia games, webisodes, and an informative "villains' gallery" of food-borne pathogens.

INDEX

A

Agricultural Research Service (ARS), 40

American Medical Association (AMA), 65

Animals
genetically modified, 84–88
use of drugs in production of, 19–20
See also Factory farms

AquaAdvantage salmon, 86–88

AquaBounty Technologies, 87–88

ARS (Agricultural Research Service), 40

ATF (Bureau of Alcohol, Tobacco, Firearms and Explosives), 42

B

Best, Jason, 84

Boner, Kayla, 45–46

Bovine spongiform encephalopathy (BSE), 25

Bureau of Alcohol, Tobacco, Firearms and Explosives (ATF), 42

C

CAFOs (Concentrated Animal Feeding Operations), 20–21
See also Factory farms

Campylobacter/campylobacteriosis, 46, 54, *56*
symptoms of, 55–56

Cantaloupes, listeria outbreak associated with, 29, *53*

Carmen, Diane, 60

Carson, Rachel, 37

CDC. *See* Centers for Disease Control and Prevention

Center for Food Safety, 84

Center for Food Safety and Applied Nutrition (CFSAN), 34

Center for Science in the Public Interest, 34, 65

Center for Veterinary Medicine (CVM), 34

Centers for Disease Control and Prevention (CDC), 23, 37
on benefits of food irradiation, 65
on campylobacter infections, 56
on *E. coli O157:H7*, 48
on industrial chemicals found in blood, 81
on listeria infections, 52
on prevalence of food-borne illness in U.S., 58, 60

CFSAN (Center for Food Safety and Applied Nutrition), 34

Clinton, Bill, 21

Food and Drug Administration,
U.S. (FDA), 14
decline in food inspections by,
34
food safety responsibilities of,
34–36
on genetically modified foods,
80–81
percentage of foreign foods
inspected by, 70
reducing industry influence over,
67
Food and Nutrition Service (FNS),
40
Food-borne illnesses, 9
annual number of cases in U.S.,
58
CDC research on, 36, 38
failure to report, 59
uncertainty in determining rates of,
49
*See also specific illnesses and
organisms*
FoodNet program, 36
Food Quality Protection Act (FQPA,
1996), 21
Food safety
CDC's role in research on, 36, 38
EPA's role in, 40–41
FDA's role in, 34–36
Federal Trade Commission's role
in, 41–42
local responsibilities for, 31–34
state responsibilities for, 34–36
USDA's role in, 39–40
ways to ensure, *38*, 62–63
Food Safety and Inspection Service

(FSIS), 39
Food Safety and Quality Assurance
(FSQA) program, 43
4-H program (USDA), 43
Fox, Nicols, 26
FQPA (Food Quality Protection
Act, 1996), 21
Fruits/vegetables, with highest/
lowest pesticide contamination,
78
FSIS (Food Safety and Inspection
Service), 39
FSQA (Food Safety and Quality
Assurance) program, 43
FTC (Federal Trade Commission),
41–42

G

Genetically modified (GM) foods, 9,
19, 80–81
benefits of, 81–82
criticisms of, 82–84
Great Depression, 16
Guillain-Barré syndrome, 55

H

HACCP (Hazard Analysis and
Critical Control Point), 27–28
Halloran, Jean, 30
Hazard Analysis and Critical
Control Point (HACCP), 27–28
HHS (U.S. Department of Health
and Human Services), 34, 36
Hudson Foods, 71

U

Union of Concerned Scientists, 67

United States
growth of agriculture in, 16–19
history of food safety in, 11–16
as percent of total world meat
consumption, 17

USDA. *See* Department of Agriculture, U.S.

W

Waldrop, Chris, 73
World Health Organization (WHO), 65
Wyatt, Dean, 67

PICTURE CREDITS

Cover : © Serenethos/ShutterStock
.com; © StudioNewmarket/Shutter
Stock.com; © Deco Images II/
Alamy

© AGStockUSA/Alamy, 75

© Alexey Stiop/ShutterStock.com, 62

© Alliance Images/Alamy, 35

© AP Images/Charles Bennett, 83

© AP Images/Ed Andrieski, 53

© AP Images/Elaine Thompson, 85

© AP Images/Kevork Djansezian, 9

© AP Images/Nati Harnik, 27, 32, 40

© Bon Appetit/Alamy, 77

© Cordelia Molloy/Photo Researchers,
Inc., 66

© Daniel Pepper/Getty Images, 20, 64

© David R. Frazier Photolibrary, Inc./
Alamy, 22

© Edwin Remsberg/Alamy, 43

© Everett Collection/Alamy, 37

© Gale/Cengage Learning, 29, 38, 50, 61

© Gary Gardiner/Bloomberg via Getty
Images, 47

© Hazel Appleton, Health Protection
Agency Centre for Infections/Photo
Researchers, Inc., 52

© Jim West/Alamy, 80

© Justin Sullivan/Getty Images, 25

© Karen Bleier/AFP/Getty Images, 41

© keith morris/Alamy, 49

© Medical-on-Line/Alamy, 56

© Monkey Business Images/Shutter
Stock.com, 78

© Nelson Ching/Bloomberg via Getty
Images, 70

© North Wind Picture Archives/
Alamy, 13

© Pete Souza/White House/Handout/
The White House/Corbis, 72

© Ryan Kelly/Congressional Quarterly/
Getty Images, 69

© Stock Connection Blue/Alamy, 18

ABOUT THE AUTHOR

Kevin Hillstrom is an independent scholar who has written extensively on health and environmental issues. His works include *U.S. Health Policy and Politics: A Documentary History* (2011).